The Person of Jesus Christ

H. R. MACKINTOSH

The Person of
Jesus Christ

Edited by
T. F. TORRANCE

T&T CLARK
EDINBURGH

T&T CLARK LTD
59 GEORGE STREET
EDINBURGH EH2 2LQ
SCOTLAND

www.tandtclark.co.uk

The Person of Jesus Christ
first published in 1912 by the Student Christian Movement
This edition first published 2000

ISBN 0 567 08695 X

British Library Cataloguing-in-Publication Data
A catalogue record for this book is available from the British Library

Typeset by Waverley Typesetters, Galashiels
Printed and bound in Great Britain by Bell & Bain Ltd, Glasgow

Contents

FOREWORD

T. F. Torrance   vii

THE PERSON OF JESUS CHRIST

Preface   3

I The Jesus of History   7

II The Christ of Experience   27

III Jesus Christ and God   49

APPRECIATION

Hugh Ross Mackintosh
Theologian of the Cross
T. F. Torrance   71

Foreword

This book represents a republication of several addresses delivered by Professor H. R. Mackintosh at a summer conference of the Student Christian Movement at Swanwick, Derbyshire, in July 1911. They were reproduced verbatim in *The Student Movement* for October, November, and December of that year, and were felt by many people to be so valuable as to make it advisable to print them in some more permanent and accessible form. They were then entirely re-written by the author, and published by the SCM in 1912.

They constitute the inner evangelical heart of his great work, *The Doctrine of the Person of Jesus Christ*, published in Edinburgh that same year by T&T Clark Ltd in their International Theological Library, and which as such has been republished again and again. That is one of the really great works in Christian Dogmatics, in which Mackintosh sought to put into historical and lucid conceptual form the truth of the biblical and doctrinal teaching about the Lord Jesus Christ as incarnate Son of God and Saviour of the world.

This little book *The Person of Jesus Christ*, is a devotional and doctrinal gem which in its direct, simple form deserves to be brought into print once again, for it will meet the spiritual needs of many Christian people today who hunger for clear, definite, uplifting teaching about the Lord Jesus, which is easily understood and directed to their personal lives.

Of particular importance for Professor Mackintosh was the statement by Jesus, recorded in slightly different words by the Evangelists: "All things are delivered unto me of my Father: and no man knoweth the Son, save but the Father; neither doth any know the Father, save the Son, and he to whomsoever the Son willeth to reveal him." Those words, Mackintosh held to be the most important for the doctrine of Christ in the New Testament, for they spoke of the unqualified correlation of the Father and the Son in being and act. The Father is personally in the Son, and the Son is personally in the Father. And so he pointed to the august and profound words of the Fourth Gospel reflecting the words of Jesus; "I and my Father are one." "He who has seen me has seen the Father." Because the Son and the Father are one in being and act, Mackintosh could even speak of "the sacrifice of the Father" in the atoning sacrifice of Jesus upon the cross, in which the Holy Spirit fully shared in his intercession for us, of which St. Paul spoke in the eighth chapter of the Epistle to the Romans about what Mackintosh called "the subduing magnitude of the Divine sacrifice".

Mackintosh's appreciation of that biblical truth constitutes the inner core of his little book, which he expounds in arguments of persuasive beauty and always closely related to Christian experience. Throughout it, without recourse to technical theological terms, he presents the evangelical heart of the historical creeds of the Church, not least their formulation of the oneness in being and saving activity between Jesus Christ and God the Father. This is a manual to which people may often turn and find nourishment for Christian belief and experience in the world today.

Such is the wholeness and integrity of the book as it was written that, save for a few minor corrections, I have preferred to let the original words stand, and not to attempt to modernize the style, nor for example to render all language "inclusive" as Mackintosh most certainly intended. Although he directs his discussion and presentation to the thinking of people in his own day, *The Person of Jesus Christ* is an unusual work that is not conditioned by time or culture, and continues to speak to us today of the atonement which God has provided for us out of his own life, and of the kind of union with Christ in which that atoning life continues to be mediated to us.

I myself have read this little book again and again, always with spiritual uplift in a quickening of my faith and deepening of my daily prayer. It is a sublime and commanding little book which it is a privilege to make available to others.

THOMAS F. TORRANCE

The Person of Jesus Christ

Preface

The following pages are an attempt to consider what is perhaps the most urgent religious question of our time – Who was Jesus Christ, and what can be definitely ascertained as to the purpose of his life? No subject could be more arresting; indeed, for earnest observers of society, none could be more vividly engrossing at the present hour. The world can hardly contain the books which are being written about Jesus. Not long since the present writer had occasion to read an article on Jesus, in a scholarly new Encyclopedia of Religion, the author of which, coming finally to mention the best literature, protested that out of the vast multitude of books he could name only an insignificant and fragmentary selection. Then two closely-printed columns were filled with books of all sorts and sizes – biographies of Jesus, controversial treatises, special studies, books on the words of Jesus, on the character of Jesus, on his life, on his birth, on his death and resurrection – most of them published within the last eight years. Thousands of teachers teach about Jesus every day. Hundreds of preachers proclaim his Gospel. If a modern theme could be named, that theme is Jesus Christ.

The subject-matter of this inquiry may be divided into three parts. First, we shall endeavour to ascertain the most important facts known to be true regarding Jesus as he lived in Palestine. Next, we shall inquire as to the place and function filled by him in Christian experience. Finally, there remains the question – so vast and overwhelming – of his relation to Almighty God. No problems more sublime could visit the human mind; yet none are so intensely practical. For none could spring more directly out of our personal attitude to the Gospel. We all of us know much regarding Jesus, and what we know is our best possession; for no man who has once absorbed a ray of Christ's light can ever again become as though he had not heard his name. At the same time, we may not as yet have focalized our impressions; we may have delayed, so far, to gather what we believe in one supreme, measured, and coherent conviction, for which we can make a stand, and which will satisfy the just demands of intellectual consistency. It is to such an inquiry, and to such an at least partial formulation of conclusions, that we are invited in the present study.

At the very outset, however, it is necessary to repeat a familiar caution, or rather perhaps to realize freshly the glory of a great promise. Our insight into the fact of Jesus will depend essentially on our spiritual attitude and temper. This is one chief matter, indeed, which is covered by the word of Jesus, "If any man willeth to do his will, he shall know of the teaching, whether it be of God" (St. John vii. 17). Instinctively we recognize that the significance of Christ is not equally clear to every one, is not in fact at all times equally clear to ourselves. Nor ought we to suppose that our appreciation of him is at all singular in this respect. The principle holds everywhere. Obedience is *always* the organ of spiritual knowledge. Is it not a familiar fact that our assurance of immortality wavers and flickers in secret concord with our habits? Does not our sense of God wax and wane with our loyalty to duty and our practice of secret prayer? So is it with the apprehension of Jesus Christ; we may make it feebly dim or grandly and inspiringly and self-evidently clear by the attitude we take to his claim upon our lives. It is right that this should be emphasized at the beginning. For it is useless to ignore the truth that the man who has no wish to be good will tell you, if he is candid, that for him Jesus Christ has no value or attractiveness of any kind. Christ means something great, something overwhelming, something divine and all-sufficient only for the man who is dissatisfied with himself; who has aimed at righteousness, and now, to his shame and grief, stands self-convicted of failure. You cannot see the beauty or the sense of the glowing cathedral window from without; to behold the splendour and the miracle you must stoop and enter: and in like manner Christ remains unintelligible and valueless to all save those who, under the constraint of righteousness, have dared to pass with him into the sanctuary of conscience. To know for certain who Christ is, we must first have gathered ourselves up in a genuine moral effort and been brave enough to look straight and clear at the facts of our own character and of the moral universe.

I

The Jesus of History

The self-consciousness of Jesus – his thought of himself, that is, and of his redeeming mission to the world – is not merely the greatest fact which concerns him; it is the greatest fact in all history. It is from this point, therefore, that we ought to start. It is the obviously right point of departure, since it furnishes at the very outset the foot-hold we require in the known actualities of the past. Not to build up an edifice of speculation is our aim, for that could only have the value and credibility of fallible human logic; but rather to account, reasonably and worthily, for the astounding circumstance that this Man holds, and has always held, the central place in the supreme religion of the world. To this starting-point there is just one possible objection, based on the hypothesis that Jesus lived under a sheer delusion about himself because he had taken up certain grandiose but pathetically absurd notions current in his own day and thus came to regard his own Person as the fulfilment of fantastic Jewish anticipations of a Saviour from heaven, while the disciples fell, so completely under his influence that, like the followers of the Mahdi, they came to share the hallucination. But this theory need not be considered seriously. In itself it is manifestly no more than a wild guess, utterly out of keeping with Jesus' acknowledged sanity and insight. Not only so; to admit that it raises a real problem is equivalent to renouncing the attitude even of moral reverence for Jesus. We could no longer venerate one whose life was built round a pure mistake.

It is right to emphasize at the outset immense significance of the fact that Jesus Christ should have had an absorbing consciousness of himself, or rather of God and himself as bound up together. No man in his senses would dream of employing the phrase "God and I", yet just this is Jesus' tone. He cannot think of himself without thinking also of God who sent him and who is perpetually with him. Still more amazing, he cannot think of God but that his mind instantly settles on himself as God's indispensable organ and representative. "My Father worketh hitherto, and I work" (St. John v. 17). Here comes the strange note of "God and I", which we should feel it impossible to adopt, or even to imitate. And it is not merely that his tone and attitude is in these ways so different from ours; it is wholly unlike anything to be found elsewhere in religious history. Take Buddha. When Buddha dies, he gives instructions that his disciples may forget him if only they remember his teaching and the way that he has shown them. Or, again, take Socrates. What he is concerned about at the end is the truth he has given his life to elucidate. These two, it has been rightly observed, are nearer to Jesus in moral power and originality than is any other; Plato speaks of Socrates,

8

in the closing lines of the *Phaedo*, as the wisest and justest and best of all men he has known; yet it is clear that it had not occurred to them to take a central position in the affections and thoughts of mankind. How different is it with Jesus! He came to lead men to God; and yet, as Herrmann has expressed it, "He knows no more sacred task than to point them to his own Person." Such was his confidence in his power to redeem, whether from sin or death, that he felt at liberty to thrust himself thus deliberately on the world's attention. The Gospel could be uttered only in this way. The good news for a world of impotence and misery could not be proclaimed save by fixing men's eyes upon himself. When therefore we repair first of all to the self-revelation of Jesus, we are standing beside the very fountain-head of all Christian religion.

The content of Jesus' self-consciousness is of course infinitely profound and comprehensive, but for our present purpose it may be most easily considered under two main aspects or divisions. In the first place, he definitely took the rôle of Messiah; in the second place, he claimed to be the Son of God.

In regard to the first point – the Messiahship of Jesus – one can almost hear the instinctive expostulation of the modern man who is conscious of living in the twentieth century. "To me", he will say, "The word 'Messiah' means nothing. It is an old Jewish word. Once, no doubt, it was filled with the life-blood of a great patriotism, but it is bleached white now." Most of us probably will understand this objection to the word, and may indeed sympathize with it. Yet after all we are here dealing not with words but with things; and what must therefore be pointed out is that whereas the mere word is old and empty, the thing is eternal. For Jesus and his countrymen, no single word had such a burning intensity of meaning as "Messiah". In claiming to be Messiah, indeed, he simply used a Jewish term expressive of his place as Saviour of the world. For what did Messiahship imply? One thing is quite certain: it did not imply anything easy, obvious, or commonplace. So far from that, its significance, is final, awful, revolutionary. To put it briefly: in Jesus' mind, as in the mind of every pious Jew, the Messiah was the Person in whom all the purposes of God were gathered up and consummated. The last foundations of being were in him. All creation in heaven and on earth, all the Divine ways of history, all time and all eternity – they meet and converge in this one transcendent Figure. Whoever turned out to be Messiah would thereby be constituted the hinge and pivot of the universe, the Person on whom everything turned in the relation of God to man. Do you imagine these are claims to be lightly raised? Are they claims, moreover, which one like Jesus would make at random? And yet, knowing this to be the meaning of the name, Jesus stood up and applied it directly to himself. I am he, he said; I am the Sent of God, in whom every promise is answered and every human prayer fulfilled.

At once we can see how tremendously it matters whether this transcendent belief about himself was or was not true. Suppose it true; then we must come to a personal understanding with Jesus regarding his significance for our own lives. It sets us right in view of the last and highest moral responsibility. It compels us to choose, to be for or against, to face toward God in Christ or away from him. Suppose it false and mistaken, what then? Can we continue to reverence the man who was deceived? Remember, this claim of Jesus has gone through history like a sword, dividing households cruelly, producing martyrdom and self-sacrifice on a scale never before seen, drawing passionate faith and love and hope from a million hearts in every generation; well, then, if it is all a mistake – if some one has blundered, and that some one Jesus – can this leave us admiring him any longer? I will go further: must it not even shake our trust in God? For consider the question yet once more in its sharpest form. Here is the most influential Figure in history, whose influence bids fair to endure as long as the world itself; and we can see that for his own mind the Messianic thought, with its boundless implications, is vital and decisive. Now confront this with the supposed fact that the belief is only a rather discreditable piece of fanaticism. What light is flung thereby on the divine government of the world? What sort of universe is it in which such things can be, in which the best and bravest and highest flows thus from a mere hallucination? Surely in view of such issues it is not too much to say that *everything* in Christian religion hangs on the spiritual veracity of Jesus' profession of Messiahship. The question is not peripheral; it is central and supreme.

To proceed then: it was this controlling conscious-ness of being *sent*, sent by God as absolute Deliverer, which interprets all the greatest facts in our Lord's career. That career was no irresponsible adventure; behind each word, act, or movement lay the vast background of a Messianic commission to mankind. In the first place, this explains *his amazing tone of moral authority*. If familiarity had not dulled our feelings as we peruse the Gospels, we should be unable to restrain our astonishment at the sense of unprecedented and inimitable authority which is manifest in Jesus. Obviously he had no scruple in asking men for unreserved loyalty to himself. He tells them that they are to give up everything, to give it up at once, to rise without a word and follow him. Nothing must be allowed to interfere with this, not even the dearest ties of natural affection. "If any man cometh unto me and hateth not his own father and mother, yea, and his own life also, he cannot be my disciple" (St. Luke xiv. 26). Not that it was a self-regarding claim. Jesus calls no man that he may use him as a tool. He has evidently no will of his own except to do what is requisite for his appointed mission; but the arresting fact is this, that he, the Meek and Lowly of heart, should conceive that mission as so bound up with his own Person as to be unrealizable apart from him. To refuse him is to forfeit eternal life; he has therefore no option but to insist on submission and obedience. We must take up our cross behind him: there is no other way. How vivid, solemn, and transfixing are the words! How they force us, if we have any seriousness of purpose, to scrutinize anew this Person who tells us that to live rightly is to accept his yoke; tells us so, indeed, as if nothing else were conceivable. Could he dare to press our conscience so hard, if he were merely one of ourselves, a pious, good man like a thousand others? There are those who skate across this problem easily, one had almost said with levity. Yet it insists on being met and solved. If Jesus was but one more human unit, however noteworthy, is this tone of ethical supremacy justified? Is it even tolerable? Is it not, rather, an outrage alike on conscience and on truth? Here, then, we realize once more, at a crucial point, how vast are the moral interests bound up with the self-consciousness of Christ. No man can read the Gospels without becoming sensible that according to our Lord's own conviction he was bringing those to whom he spoke into the presence of the final moral obligation; with the consequence that their attitude to him could be no question of taste, or accident, or degree; it was a question, rather, of life and death. We have only to face frankly the moral authority of Christ, alone with conscience and in a still hour, to have the staggering conviction thrust upon us that in truth this Man has a right to the Name which is above every name.

The next fact made luminous by Jesus' consciousness of himself is *his forgiveness of sin*. When we read that marvellous episode in Mark ii., the healing of the paralytic – one of the most significant passages in all the Gospels – we are at once struck by the fact that Jesus does not proclaim forgiveness merely (which any Christians may do, and all Christians ought to); *he professes to impart it*. He puts forgiveness, you may say, right into the sufferer's heart; and when challenged as to his prerogative, he replies by a miracle of healing. Doubtless it may be said that in a real sense we also forgive sin. In St. John's Gospel we have the risen Lord's promise or declaration: "Whose soever sins ye forgive, they are forgiven unto them; whose soever sins ye retain, they are retained" (xx. 23). But observe the difference. When we proclaim pardon to sinful men – whether from the pulpit or in fireside talk – we do it in view of Jesus, the guarantee of Divine grace to all the guilty; when Jesus offers pardon in the Gospels, it is in virtue of himself. Not as though he expected men to believe it apart from what they knew of *him*. As it has been put: "Jesus did not write the story of the Prodigal Son on a sheet of paper for those who knew nothing of himself. He told it to men who saw him, and who, through all that he was, were assured of the Father in heaven, of whom he was speaking." These guilty men found pardon realized in Jesus; as he stood before them, he was surety to their souls of the forgiving love of God. The woman that was a sinner (Luke vii.) became conscious in his presence that he was the door of entrance to a purer and better life; in him, she felt, the Father said to her aching heart, "I am thy salvation." If till then God had been a name of fear, and past and present were disquieting, there now came to her, mediated by Jesus' tone and look, the blest sense of a Divine love mightier than her sin – that initial assurance of forgiveness which makes all things new. A voice said, "Rise up and be God's child"; and in that swift realization of patient love which yet would make no terms with sin, the peace of reconciliation flowed down into her soul. Thus Jesus pardoned sin.

Now it is only long familiarity which hides from us the astounding character of forgiveness. Nothing in the world is so purely supernatural; in comparison the raising of the dead may be called a trifle. Do we not feel how impossible it is to forgive ourselves if anything real has to be forgiven? Doubtless we can make an apology to our own better nature, thus wiping the offence, whatever it is, off the slate; but mere honesty will confess that really this is not forgiveness in the least. Strictly speaking, we can no more forgive ourselves than we can shake hands with ourselves or look into our own eyes. Further, we are quite well aware that although we may forgive a man the injury he has done us, we can never forgive his sin. That he must settle with Almighty God, and he knows it. But the amazing fact is that Jesus said to men: You can settle it with me. You can tell me of your penitence, and I am able to grant the Divine forgiveness. Not only did he say this; over and over again he made good his words. In unnumbered cases he lifted the burden from the bad conscience, took off the paralysing touch of guilt, and once for all flung wide the gate of righteousness to those who had bolted and barred it in their own face. He claimed to open the prison door to the captives of despair; and by a word, a look, a touch of holy love, he opened it, so that in the power of his presence men stood up, shook off their chains, and passed out *free*. We need not now pause to analyse the various implications of such an act. But anyone can see that Jesus could not have offered pardon to men in his own Person – on his own account and guarantee, as it were – if he had himself been conscious of sin; while on the other hand it is sheerly unthinkable that one such as he could have been sinful without knowing it. In the Roman service of the Mass there comes a point at which the celebrating priest, even in that awful hour, makes confession of sin to the con-gregation, begging them to pray God for him; but there is no such consciousness in Jesus. He is aware that he needs no cleansing. Even in the article of death he knows it. There is no consciousness of sin; there is no memory of sin; there is no fear of sin as a future contingency flowing from the weakness or short-coming of even the most distant past. Sinlessly one with God, all his life he moved among men, uttering the word of pardon to the guilty, and uttering it with Divine effect.

The third point which in a real sense is made intelligible by the Messianic consciousness of Jesus is *his working of miracles*. Every now and then, as we learn from history, the Church passes through a certain period when she is more or less ashamed of the miracles of Jesus; and beyond all question this is due in part to inherited misconceptions of miracle as such. It is thought to be a violation of law, a breach of causation, or the like, and not unnaturally definitions of this kind create a violent and unfavourable prejudice. But it is coming to be quite clearly understood that miracle need not imply any violation of law, and that belief in miracle is simply another name for belief in the Living God. To quote one of the most acute of British philosophers, Professor A. E. Taylor, "There is no philosophical justification for relegating the provi-dential action of God to the infinitely remote past, and refusing to admit the possibility of incessant new departures. Nor have we any ground to declare that the actual course of events is conformable to 'immut-able laws'. This has an important bearing on the reality of those unusual sequences commonly called 'miracles'. There is really no reason why the most unusual things should not be happening somewhere or other every day. In fact, the wonder would be, not that there should be 'miracles', but that there should be so few of them." If we have rejected the impossible conception of the universe as a mechanical system in which everything – including history and all human action – is absolutely and fatally determined, and if in addition to this we believe in the Living God of Jesus, we are quite at liberty to hold that miracles are both possible and real.

To return, however: my point is that whether the Church is or is not ashamed of miracles, it is at least obvious that Christ was not. On the contrary, we may affirm with all reverence that, coming forward as he did in the character of Messiah, he would have been ashamed *not* to do wondrous works. Remember once again what Messiahship implies and must imply. The Messiah came to establish the Divine rule, the Kingdom of God; to establish it in a world not of sin merely, but of need, of pain, of death, of despair. If there is one point upon which scholars are agreed to-day, it is that the Kingdom as Jesus conceived it was a new, heavenly, supernatural order of redemption, differing *toto coelo* from the old disappointing order – an order of so transcendent a character that sin and grief should be abolished within its range, and the omnipotent love of God have free play. Jesus knew that all this had been eagerly expected by the best souls in each generation, and, when he stood up to preach at Nazareth, his first word was the announcement that the expectation was now fulfilled. The saying of the French monarch is familiar: *L'état c'est moi* – Myself am the State. Take away the arrogance and falsehood, and we have precisely the message of Jesus to those who heard him: I myself am the Kingdom. God's reign is begun in my presence among you. What the miracles of Jesus meant therefore to his own mind was simply that the first dawning gleams of the new day had begun to shine. The vast novel powers of the new order, and its revolutionizing energies, were now firmly planted in the world in his Person; and as his ministry broadened out from more to more, he was conscious of his power to work what has been called "the comprehensive miracle of redemption", not only forgiving all our iniquities but healing all our diseases.

And now we come to an idea of incalculable importance for religion, although we cannot here treat of it with the proper fulness and minuteness. It is the idea of *a suffering Messiah*. The thought of a Messiah had of course been familiar for centuries, but nothing could be more misleading than to suppose that Jesus Christ simply took over the prevailing view of his day and country. He struck into a completely new line. Till then it had been believed – and the belief is still a synonym for worldliness – that the way to true sovereignty is brute force. One has only to glance at Babylonian sculpture to realize the brutal notion of lordship or supremacy which prevailed in the ancient world. Force, it appeared, was the secret of majesty and power. Did Christ therefore utterly reject the wish for power? Far from it. Instead, as the author of *Ecce Homo* has expressed it, he laid claim "persistently, with the calmness of entire conviction, in opposition to the whole religious world, in spite of the offence which his own followers conceived, to a dominion more transcendent, more universal, more complete, than the most delirious votary of glory ever aspired to in his dreams." He claimed to be King, Master, and Judge of men. He claimed this; but also he adopted the unheard-of plan of maintaining, not in theory only but in practice, that true power comes by sacrifice and pain, and for his kingly portion he chose the Cross. This, as I have said, was a gloriously new conception. No one had imagined it before, but obviously when once it is understood, it puts us right up against an insistent, stupendous problem. Where does the problem lie?

Some pages back we saw reason to believe that the person of the Messiah was the central fact in history at once the pivot and the climax of the Divine world-plan; and now we are faced by the startling circum-stance that – according to Jesus' self-description – this Messiah is to perish in a death of shame. He is to die thus mysteriously notwithstanding his incomparable greatness and innocence of life. How can this be? It need scarcely be pointed out that ordinary analogies between Jesus and ourselves are here of no avail. No general principles will suffice, and of this we are conscious in our best moments. We men and women have contributed to the world's sin; therefore, as we shall all concede, justice prescribes for us a personal share in the world's pain. Yet in the case before us, so exceptional, so unique in moral majesty and self-abnegation, in a life where sin has no part or lot, there is appointed a death of unexampled contumely and suffering. How can it be explained? The answer to this tremendous problem surely lies in a direction to which the Sufferer himself has pointed. There are two great passages in the Gospels in which our Lord's teaching on his death is recorded with entire clearness. The first is St. Mark x. 45: "Even the Son of Man came not to be ministered unto but to minister, and to give his life a ransom for many." The other is St. Mark xiv. 24, where, as he gave the cup in the Last Supper to the disciples, he said: "This is My blood of the covenant, which is shed for many." In both cases our Lord is referring to the forgiveness of sins, and what he declares plainly is that this unspeakable blessing will be gained for men at the cost of his life. If we are pardoned, we owe it to the death of Christ. His death, in other words, had reference to sin. Just because he was Messiah, the Deliverer sent of God, he must take upon him to deliver man from the sorest of all troubles. He could not bear to pass by on the other side. How or when God revealed to him that this self-identification with sinful men would lead him to the Cross, is far from easy to determine, nor indeed is it essential. But we know that his soul fed upon the Old Testament; and this being so, it is natural to think of the wonderful 53rd chapter of Isaiah as having been to Jesus the word of God calling him to his vicarious Passion. However that may be, and whatever the avenue by which he travelled, at all events he spoke the words just cited in the full, clear certitude that he must stoop to conquer; that only as "lifted up" by crucifixion could he draw all men to him. So that what Christ leaves on our mind, as we ought to note emphatically, what he leaves there as the central fact of the world, is *the Messiah dying for sin*. It is a picture and a fact which every serious man must gaze upon with all his soul and mind and strength. It is the supreme reality of human life. And it means at least this, that whereas self-consciousness in us is one of the gravest moral faults which separates us from others as by a yawning chasm, the great self-consciousness of Christ drew him so close to us that at the last his love bore our sins in death.

Of the two parts into which our present inquiry is divided, Jesus' Messiahship and his Divine Sonship, the first is now completed. We have learnt the opinion held by Jesus regarding his own mission, and we have inquired as to the bearing of his Messianic position on such things as forgiveness and the working of miracles. Let us now ask what light is cast by Jesus on *his personal relationship* to God.

As a preliminary we may remark that, if it should appear that Christ claimed to stand in a unique and incomparable relationship to God, this, in view of our former results, will be felt by reasonable men as affording relief from the gravest moral and intellectual difficulties. No doubt it seems at first only to create a fresh difficulty, since everything unique has a strong presumption against it and requires more than usually convincing proof. From a still higher point of view, however, it is obvious that Jesus' special Sonship mitigates the difficulties we have already felt in other portions of his teaching. If he stands on God's side, addressing us in God's name, it is not wonderful that he should speak in tones of moral authority, or exercise the prerogative of pardon, or present himself as bearing the world's sin in death. We can see a meaning stealing into these facts, which fall into a transparent order and fitness if we view them in the light of his higher consciousness of an unshared connexion with the Father.

Now that is precisely the word we want, the word "presuppose"; it describes more accurately than any other the real attitude of our Lord. He did not dwell upon his Sonship – I mean generally, in the Synoptic narrative; he did not make it the explicit subject of debate or argument. He assumed it rather, in word and look. But what people assume is just what they are surest of. It leaves the deepest mark on the mind of the observer, for what is done with a quiet deliberation and composure always is done with emphasis. It is thus that Jesus acts. Gradually the disciples became aware that he was taking a place beside God, a place in which he could have neither substitute nor partner. His attitude meant that he was the Person on whom everything in religion turned, completely covering and determining our relation to God. He is *the* Son distinctively; and to men he offers power to become sons of God through his mediation. In the Son the Father is revealed; and as there is but one Father, and cannot be more, so there cannot be more than one Son, supreme and absolute. "Sympathy", it has been said, "is not more a characteristic of Jesus than aloofness or reserve. However fraternal his relations with others, they were penetrated with this quality of separateness and authority." Both aspects of the total fact must be recognized. Never was there a more loving heart than Jesus, who is the Elder Brother of us all; yet nowhere, not once in all his life, do we find him stepping down and standing simply at our side. He speaks freely of "your Father", "the Father", "my Father", and in a memorable scene recorded by the fourth Evangelist, combining both modes of designation, he employs the double phrase, "My Father and your Father", in which the distinction is sustained firmly. And yet – while it is from his blessed lips we have learnt that Father is God's name – he avoids the phrase "*our* Father" with a care and (as it seems) a solemnity of omission which can scarcely have been accidental. Not only so, but in one of the best accredited parts of the tradition he is recorded to have said, "No one knoweth the Son, save the Father; neither doth any know the Father, save the Son, and he to whomsoever the Son willeth to reveal him" (St. Matt. xi. 27). I have never heard these words read aloud in public assembly, but they brought a hush upon the audience, so lofty are they, so ultimate, so inimitable and august.

This unique Sonship, it is clear from the Synoptic Gospels, formed the basis and inspiration of Jesus' life-work. It was in the strength of it, and as commissioned and authorized by it, that he accomplished his redeeming service for mankind. He came, as we have already seen, to set up the Kingdom of God's almighty and righteous love. Its establishment was the appointed task of the Messiah. But – and this a point of first-rate significance – Christ knew himself to be Messiah because deeper even than Messiah he was the Son of God. In that unshared filial life he knows God, and is known of him, in a mode which admits of no kind of comparison with other men. They are the lost children, who need the Kingdom; he is the Son who brings it in. In the secret place of the inmost self-consciousness, in the sanctuary of personal feeling, he experiences his filial unity with the Father. And therefore – to repeat it yet once more – he is sure of his equipment for the great mission. To know himself as Son is also, and simply by itself, to know himself called to make the Kingdom a reality within the world of men, to lay its eternal foundations by bringing home to men at once the Father's holy condemnation of sin and his compassionate mercy for the sinful. As the only begotten Son of God, he and he alone was able to lead lost sons back to the Father.

That all these singular professions regarding his own Person must have left a deep mark, cannot reasonably be doubted. Especially is it clear that they could not but affect, and affect profoundly, the minds and thoughts of his disciples. And when we open the New Testament, we find that it was so. No one can say "He that findeth his life shall lose it, but he that loseth his life for my sake shall find it" – no one can say such words, I repeat, without having to take the consequences; and in the case of Jesus Christ this meant that men began to trust him with the trust they gave to God. Jesus saw this; he wrought for it; he expected it; and when at last it came, he joyfully gave God thanks. The problem now remaining on our minds, therefore, is whether he was equal to the place which he had thus taken by accepting the religious faith and loyalty tendered by his followers. He had presented himself as able to save to the uttermost. And now that men turned to him with an honest and pathetic readiness to be saved, had he the power to fulfil his chosen task? He had spoken words of eternal life, and had connected them vitally with his own Person. Was he able to make these words good in the experience of believing hearts? Was he able to do for them exceeding abundantly above all that they could ask or think? To this question we now turn.

II

The Christ of Experience

In our study of the historic Jesus it has been made clear that he entertained a certain view of his own Person, and put himself forward in a quite definite religious character. He put himself forward in the specific character of Messiah – as the Deliverer, that is, sent of God to rescue man from all his sorest troubles and to bring in the new order which should fully express Almighty Love. Furthermore, he claimed to be equal to this task because in some lonely sense, and by the constitution of his being, he was the Son of God. Or, to put it otherwise, he came forth professing to be a Saviour, on the largest scale. We have now to inquire more closely whether, and how, this tremendous claim has been vindicated in human lives. Is it or is it not the fact that Jesus Christ has exerted what we must call a redeeming influence on men like ourselves? If he has, what light is thereby cast upon his Person?

It would of course be no better than affectation were we, even for the temporary purposes of argument, to regard it as an open question whether Christ does or does not save men. That he has enabled sinners to live in fellowship with God, assured them of Divine pardon, and inspired them with triumphant moral power, will probably not be denied except by those who consider spiritual experience as a whole to be illusory. For Christians, however, who cannot take this line, the redeeming might of Jesus Christ is an assured and fundamental fact; the point, indeed, is one on which they are not at liberty to pretend ignorance. They would not venture to call themselves Christians unless they felt free, or rather felt bound, to utter before him the great testimony of St. Peter: "Thou hast the words of eternal life." All this, I need hardly say, is compatible with widely-ranging differences of opinion as to the mode in which the salvation due to Christ has been effected. We must not confuse redemption as an experience with theories of its possibility. At the same time, this underlying conviction that Christ does redeem men, if held now in the foreground of our minds, will help to safeguard us from treating the present subject – our Lord's place in experience – as only an imaginary hypothesis, a curious or piquant problem on which to sharpen our wits. It is a subduing thought that all round us, at this very hour, men are being saved by Christ.

Let us realize, then, that redemption by Jesus is a fact, which we assume but do not prove. It is there, confronting us with inexpugnable reality before ever we proceed to analyse or explain it; our only task, accordingly, is to ascertain precisely what it consists in, and to what high issues it moves. Its actuality in this experimental sense, however, proves at the very outset that Jesus' witness to himself, as already considered, was neither rash nor baseless. His promise is seen to be well-grounded in reality. The profession of Redeemership made by him, and on the other hand the human experience that he redeems, appear like the curves of a noble arch rising up in lofty sweep to meet and join.

Time would fail were we to expatiate at length on what Jesus Christ is known to have accomplished in those lives which have received him by obedient trust. That is an unending story. We are all aware that if any truth resides in the higher human testimony; unless people have conspired strangely to talk cant, without any concrete or intelligible motive but in many instances with the sole result of incurring loss, persecution, and even death itself, Christ has transformed their lives. Men and women like ourselves have been re-created by his influence, changed in the depths and inmost secrets of being. In every man that change takes a different, because a personal, shape. His redemption is as original and individual a fact as the colour of his eyes. Each rising sun, touching the wing of sleeping birds, wakes over the woods a fresh burst of melody, as if the sun had never risen before; and just so, wherever a man finds and grasps redemption, faith in the heart is a new creation, as if he were the first to discover Jesus. Nevertheless, since human nature is after all a unity, through all this wonderful and incalculable variety there run certain well-marked lines of resemblance, certain uniformities of response to Christ and of benefit received from him. Let us select one or two of these for closer scrutiny. We shall not exhaust the subject, but we may hope to see how inexhaustible it is.

First, then, as a cardinal certainty we take *the felt presence of Jesus Christ with men.* Since our Lord lived in Palestine, there has been an innumerable company of believers, who are sensible that he is theirs with so intimate a nearness that they can hold fellowship with him, can really possess him as an indwelling and controlling life. The late Dr. Jowett, of Balliol, who held no brief for orthodoxy, speaks in language of haunting beauty on this subject. He points to "the knowledge and love of Christ, by which men pass out of themselves to make their will his and his theirs, the consciousness of him in their thoughts and actions, communion with him, and trust in him. Of every act of kindness or good which they do to others his life is the type; of every act of devotion or self-denial his death is the type; of every act of faith his resurrection is the type. *And often they walk with him on earth, not in a figure only, and find him near them, not in a figure only, in the valley of death.* They experience from him the same kind of support as from the sympathy and communion of an earthly friend. That friend is also a Divine power."

It may be there is something in this language which goes beyond the experience of many Christians. Yet, on the other hand, when men speak of fellowship with Christ, be it in living or in dying, they are not using highly coloured metaphors; they are not indulging in the impatient hyperbole we employ so often when excited or hard pressed in argument; they are merely and simply reporting one of the most real elements of their personal existence. They mean a Presence, unseen yet unknown, which impinges on their lives day after day and hour by hour; a Presence which, if they wished to be rid of it, they would have to exert force to thrust away. To this there is no proper analogy elsewhere. Doubtless it is often said that the spirit of Lord Salisbury or Mr. Gladstone still abides with the great political party of which each was acknowledged leader; but whatever be the truth in this form of expression, it is used, quite certainly, with a clear consciousness of its fundamentally figurative character. Thus instinctively we speak of these great statesmen as *departed*; but Christians of the type I have referred to could not consent to speak of a departed Lord. Again, when we remember dear familiar friends now with God, we remember them as they were, in their form and habit as they once lived; but the Christ with whom believing men hold communion now is not merely the Jesus who walked in Palestine; he is the exalted Lord, present with his people in the sovereign power of his resurrection and as inhabiting a higher order than that of time and space. And once more, we do not feel that anything in the present influence of our departed friends, and our response to it, is determining our relation to God. Yet this precisely is what we feel in regard to Christ. Our attitude to him, and his unimaginable love to us, affects our relation to the Father in a profound and decisive manner. He gives to us the life of God; he constantly renews, sustains, and augments it.

From the beginning until now, there have been those who denied this unseen but real presence of Christ. A man may quite sincerely say, "I am at a loss to understand, when you speak of Christ's continual nearness to us; for myself, I am unconscious of anything of that sort." Plainly, however, this objection may be taken from various points of view. Thus the objector may not himself claim to be a Christian. In that case, it will probably be agreed his position need cause no surprise, since only Christians can have the authentic Christian experience. It would, indeed, be surprising were it otherwise; the really disconcerting and unintelligible thing would be to find that a man could actually have the Christian experience without wishing for it, or even knowing it – like measles. Not only so; but though he may be a true Christian, it does not follow that he will have realized at the very outset the deepest and richest elements in Christianity. Elsewhere in human life, certainly, we allow for wide margins of nobler attainment. When a boy wakens to the beauty and the charm of Nature, do we suppose that *at once* her sublimer secrets will unfold, that at once he will understand the lines –

> Two voices are there; one is of the sea,
> One of the mountains; each a mighty voice?

Could one whose sense of poetic power had been faintly stirred by Scott's *Marmion* claim to appreciate from the very outset all that Shakespeare, Milton, Wordsworth, have done for men? In such cases we refuse, and rightly refuse, to pare down the significance of the greatest things to some poor minimum or insipid average; for we are conscious that within the infinite experience of poetic feeling abundant room is given for growth, enrichment, expansion. There is a progress from more to more, as men "follow on to know". Similarly in the religious field there are degrees in our appreciation of redemption; and every one who clearly recalls his own past is aware that, if he has honestly given the Gospel a chance, there has been recognizable though inter-mittent progress in his certainty as to the greatness and the love of Jesus Christ. We must not then too hastily conclude that a conception like personal fellowship with Christ is an imaginative but unreal addition to the original simplicities of mere obedience to his commands. Not only does it remain a problem whether we *can* keep his commandments save as united to him spiritually; but it is an obviously just principle that the question how much the Gospel offers us is to be answered, not by a scrutiny of the partial attainments or discoveries we have so far made, but by consideration of the promises held forth by Christ, as well as the believing experience of past ages. In any case, let us decline to measure the potencies of the Christian life by the meagrest and least daring standard. Let us hope for nothing lower than the Best from the God and Father of Jesus.

No one can read modern literature on the origins of Christianity without recognizing that in a certain type of book this thought of Christ's unseen presence is wholly lacking. What we find, rather, is an attempt to put Jesus back firmly into the first century, hold him a prisoner there, and draw a line round him (as it were) beyond which his personal activities must not be permitted to extend. Is he more than a dead Jew, who perished about A.D. 30? Now, when we look away from books to actual life, we discover that Christ remains past *only as long as he is not faced in the light of conscience.* So long as we bring into play our intellect merely, or the reconstructive fancy of the historian, he is still far off; we need not even hold him at arm's length; he is not close to us at all. The change comes when we take up the moral issue. If we turn to him as men keen to gain the righteous, overcoming life, but conscious so far of failure, instantly he steps forward out of the page of history, a tremendous and exacting reality. We cannot read his greatest words, whether of command or promise, without feeling, as it has been put, that "he not only said these things to men in Palestine, but is saying them to ourselves now". He gets home to our conscience in so direct a fashion – even when we do not wish to have anything to do with him – that we feel and touch him as a present fact. Like any other fact, he can of course be kept out of our mind by the withdrawal of attention. But once he has obtained entrance, and, having entered, has shown us all things that ever we did, he moves imperiously out of the distant years into the commanding place in consciousness now and here. We cross the watershed, in fact, between a merely past and a present Christ, when we have courage to ask, not only what we think of him, but what he thinks of us. For that is to bring the question under the light of conscience, with the result that his actual moral supremacy, his piercing judgment of our lives, now becomes the one absorbing fact. His eyes seem to follow us, like those of a great portrait. When men accept or reject him, they do so to his face.

But more. Do we sufficiently realize the master force which has sustained the saints of God in their darkest hours? Take the Christian workers in our slums, in the rookeries of our large towns; take the missionaries in

Uganda or Manchuria or the far South Seas. What power enables them to endure not with persistence merely, but with cheerfulness? Can we doubt the answer? Think of those Uganda boys, told of in the Life of Hannington, who, when burned in martyrdom, praised Jesus in the fire, "singing", as the biographer has said, "till their shrivelled tongues refused to form the sound" –

> Daily, daily, sing to Jesus,
> Sing, my soul, his praises due,
> *All he does* deserves our praises,
> And our deep devotion too.

Or take an incident like the following: – The University of Glasgow conferred upon David Livingstone the degree of Doctor of Laws on his return after being in Africa sixteen years. The students, bent on fun, were in the gallery, armed with sticks, pea-shooters, and other instruments for assisting their natural powers of making themselves disagreeable. Livingstone appeared gaunt and wrinkled after twenty-seven fevers, darkened by the sun, and with an arm hanging useless, from a lion's bite. The pea-shooters ceased firing, and all felt instinctively that fun should not be poked at such a man. Livingstone was allowed to speak without interruption. He said that he would go back to Africa to open fresh fields for British commerce, to suppress the slave trade, and to propagate the Gospel of Christ. He referred proudly to the honourable careers of many who had been with him in college, and with sadness to the fate of some who had gone wrong. "'Shall I tell you', he asked, 'what sustained me amidst the toil, and hardship, and loneliness of my exiled life? It was the promise, "Lo, I am with you always, even unto the end."' The effect which the words had, coming unexpectedly from one who was both the witness and example of the promise, could not have been surpassed since they were first uttered in Galilee."[1] The incident is suggestive on another ground. It indicates that the certainty of Christ's sustaining power rests not on individual conviction merely, but on the Lord's own promise. He *undertook* to give those who trusted him this enduring spiritual presence and power. As it has been put in a well-known and exceptionally clear-sighted book: "Jesus exerted a marvellous spiritual influence by his personality during his life, but, as that earthly life was drawing to its close, we do not find him contemplating the withdrawal or diminution of that influence. The very contrary. He promised its persistence and even its augmentation. That very spirit with which he had baptized men, and which it only too inevitably seemed must pass with his earthly presence, is the very thing which most impressively, he declared would be given more than ever. By this spirit, he clearly meant certainly nothing less than all that his present personality had been; and indeed, his meaning he often simply expressed by saying that he – all that the personal contact with himself had meant – would not pass. It is this note which is the most remarkable characteristic of the latter phases of the utterances of Jesus. There is nothing like it in the later teaching of any other man."[2]

[1] Hardy, *Doubt and Faith*, pp. 174–75.
[2] Simpson, *The Fact of Christ*, pp. 73–74.

The words of Christ, then, echoed by our experience of their fulfilment, prove that belief in his constant presence is no fiction.

It is of course an easy thing to ask difficult philosophic questions regarding the abiding nearness of the Lord. A child of three will often ask questions about God and man, heaven and earth, which no living man can solve; when the mind is dealing with an infinite object, it will always be so. But these subtler problems lie beyond our present aim. We are merely registering the experience of Christian men; and it is a mere fact that at this hour there are thousands to whom the felt presence of Christ is as real as the consciousness of right and wrong. Surely we cannot refrain from seeking an explanation of this extraordinary Person who is still close to his disciples. Who is he? Whence has he come? How is it that death did not silence and remove him as it has silenced all the rest? We have no choice but to try and clear up our minds. When the Church did that, she made the Creeds; and we well know where she set him in the great confessions of her faith. If any one objects to Creeds, there is no reason at all why they should not be put aside for the time being, provided we replace them by two books which make a tolerably good substitute – the New Testament and the hymn-book. The simple fact that New Testament believers prayed to Christ sufficiently demonstrates what they held true regarding his personal spiritual presence. And when we scan a great Christian hymn like "Jesu, Lover of my soul", the witness borne by what has been called "the layman's manual of theology" –

the hymn-book – stands out with the same decisive evidence.

Let us now turn to *the conquest of sin attained through Christ*. As an element in experience this is as indubitable as the other, and it lights up his Person no less strikingly.

Sin is conquered in two ways. It is conquered first and foremost when God destroys its power to exclude us from his fellowship: or, in plain English, its back is broken when we know ourselves forgiven and thus gain a great initial assurance of the Divine love which enables us to make a start in the Christian life and to do something like justice to the Gospel. Once we know that God is ours, and that he pledges himself to keep us his, we can put up a good fight; for now sin is under our feet, and what remains is only that by God's help we should steadily crush its life out. This is essential to all true and triumphant conflict. Where do we receive this impression of forgiveness, on which everything depends? Men do not gather it out of the air. It is as far as possible from being a commonplace. On the contrary, it has come to all who now possess it in a quite specific way; it has come to them in the presence of Jesus Christ and very specially in the presence of his Cross. For there we confront the full expression of God's mind both to sinners and to sin.

Consider the man who is standing before the Cross, with soul laid open in humility to its impression. What does he feel? Two things certainly. First, he feels that sin is condemned there – condemned absolutely, for good and all. Place yourself before the dying Christ, and at once you become aware that through Jesus' eyes, as we behold his death, there looks out upon us, with humbling and convicting power, the very holiness of God with which evil cannot dwell. Never was sin so exposed, and, by exposure, so doomed, reprobated, sentenced, as by his treatment of it from the beginning to the end. When Christ had done with sin, it stood there a beaten, powerless thing; paralysed, vanquished, dethroned, stripped of every covering, every mask, flung out in utter degradation. Now as we feel his look upon us, under the shadow of the Cross, he is doing this still, doing it to us. The voice of his passion condemns our evil; but in its unheard tones there is audible the voice of God. In virtue of his oneness with the Father, Christ declares and brings home to conscience the final truth regarding the sinfulness of sin. He forgives our trespass only because in God's name and with God's authority he has first passed judgment on it from which there is no appeal.

This is the first strain we may distinguish in feeling, but it is not alone. Beside it, or rather interwoven and suffused with it, is the feeling also that there is love in the Cross; love beyond all we could ask or think. It was for love that Jesus died. And let us not miss the wonder of the circumstance that this dying love is felt as *the love of God himself*. Actually, literally, and just as we experience it, it is the love of the Eternal. It is God who in Jesus meets us, evoking faith, calming fear, cleansing conscience; giving us, as Bunyan puts it, "rest by his sorrow and life by his death". If the Cross means redemption, then it is by God himself and none other that the price of redemption has been paid. In what he undergoes on Calvary Jesus is not merely pointing upward to a Divine love beyond and above his own person, a love which he does no more than announce; he is bringing it in upon our soul. He puts it in our hand as we survey the despised shame, and as we gaze on him there comes home to us the inexpressible pathos and sacrifice of the words: "He that spared not his own Son, but delivered him up for us all." The passion of God is there. When we drop the sounding line in that sea, we hear the lead plunge down into unfathomable waters.

Is it too much to say that Jesus' dying love is itself the love of God? Surely not. Let us ask why the Cross of Christ does not revolt us. Why, in view of that ineffable Passion, do we not cry shame against the government of the world? Why is it not felt as the most insuperable of difficulties by all who attempt to justify the ways of God to men? For here is the best and holiest Soul of history, whom we dare not praise because he is above all praise; yet his career and his end are such that we still name him "the Man of Sorrows". Why do our hearts not flame with indignation against God himself that this should have been Christ's appointed lot? Because we feel, even if it be dimly, that the love which meets us there and endures all for our sake is veritably the personal love of God. Christ is not a good man merely, whom God seized and made an example of for all time; in his life, rather, the Love that is supreme has stooped down to suffer in behalf of men. This and nothing else has broken the world's hard heart. What might and must have been the worst of perplexities is all transcended, if we but catch the pure shining in it of the divine mercy in such an intensity of revelation as solves all difficulties and calms all fears. Now, as Luther said, "we have a gracious God". The Cross is a casement opening on a new world.

> The very God! think Abib; dost thou think?
> So, the All-Great, were the All-Loving too –
> So, through the thunder comes a human voice
> Saying, "O heart I made, a heart beats here!
> Face, my hands fashioned, see it in myself!
> Thou hast no power nor mayst conceive of mine,
> But love I gave thee, with myself to love,
> And thou must love me who have died for thee."

So much, then, for forgiveness. The second mode in which sin is overcome is by the breaking of its tyranny in character. Not only is pardon mediated to us by a Christ who loves while he condemns – expiating sin that he may be able to forgive it – but also it is Jesus Christ who gives power over evil habit. In the field of religious experience there is no point as to which so wide and joyous unanimity prevails as in regard to the moral inspiration and triumphant energy that flow from Christ to tempted men. People like us have been saved by him; saved not in a vague or unverifiable sense, but saved from contempt, saved from despair, saved into freedom to stop sinning, saved into the successful pursuit of goodness and likeness to the Father. The glorious fact, thanks be to God, is being repeated every day. Men who have lost faith in aspiration, whose friends have given them up in sheer disgust or in sad weariness, encounter something or some one that persuades them to commit their lives to Jesus Christ; with what effect? With this effect, that instantly or by degrees new life is imparted to them, new tastes, hopes, preferences, inclinations, motives, delights; until not in boasting but for sheer thankfulness they dare to say: "I can do all things through Christ that strengtheneth me." Christ keeps what we entrust to him. I can still hear the tones of Professor Henry Drummond's voice, twenty years ago, in those wonderful Edinburgh University meetings, as he explained what Christ would do for us. "I cannot guarantee", he would say, "that the stars will shine brighter when you leave this hall to-night, or that when you wake to-morrow a new world will open before you. But I do guarantee that Christ will keep that which you have committed to him. He will keep his promise, and you will find something real and dependable to rely on and to lead you away from documental evidence to him who speaks to your heart at this moment." And it has come true, every word. In our time it has come true as in the times before us, exactly as Christ said. "He that followeth me shall not walk in darkness, but shall have the light of life." Always, everywhere, it is found that those who answer his demand receive his promise. The power of Jesus Christ to produce and sustain character, then, is an experimental fact as well-grounded as the law of gravitation. For those who cast themselves on him, in faith's great venture, accepting honourably the conditions under which alone spiritual truth can be verified, the truth becomes luminous and certain. They discover that to be Christians is not to repeat a creed, or to narrow life into a groove; but to have a strong, patient, divine Leader, whom they can trust perfectly and love supremely, who is always drawing out in them their true nature and making them resolve to be true to it through the future; who looks into their eyes when they betray him, making them ashamed, who imparts the forgiveness of sins and gives power to live in fellowship with God. Apart from this, his call would only mean a new despair. But his strength is made perfect in weakness.

Is not all this the token of something unique and superhuman in his Person? Could a man who had perished in the first century inspire us thus? Could he support us in the conflict with self and evil by his sympathy and communion? Could he dwell within us, possessing will and heart? Surely to think so is to play with words. For we know what man can do, and also what he cannot. If we search for words to express the absolute unity of God with man, we light inevitably on some such words as we have employed regarding Jesus Christ. If God were to come in person by incarnation, by personal presence, are not these the very signs, the authentic powers, by which his glorious advent might be known?

Finally, in Christ we have *a perfect revelation of God the Father*. This comes appropriately at the point we have now reached, since it is always through redemption as an experience that revelation is vouchsafed. Through Christ the Saviour we see back into the Father's heart from which he came.

Now we may lay hold of this principle by either of two handles; it scarcely matters which. Of course it is unquestionable that men may find *some* thought of God elsewhere than in Christ. To deny that would be monstrous. For example, it was not reserved for Jesus to reveal God as Creator or Sustainer of the world; ages ere he came, these stupendous truths had become the possession of many a heart, bringing light and calm. It was not reserved for Jesus to make God known as supreme Moral Authority; this conviction also had been attained. It *was* reserved for him to manifest God in the character of loving and holy Fatherhood, *a Fatherhood which embraces all the world*. History teaches that men cannot come, and never have come, to a distinct impression of the Fatherhood of God, in the loftiest and most subduing sense, save through Jesus Christ. "Neither doth any know *the Father*, save the Son"; "No man cometh unto *the Father* but by Me" – these august words are confirmed by the facts of life. But not in words merely was the great revelation given. The life of Jesus, as it moved onward, was a ceaseless proclamation of the novel thought of God. For the first time it was shown how God loves each individual life, seeking the lost untiringly and counting no price too great for their recovery. Nowhere does Jesus take this message into the atmosphere of theory; he is content that it should rest in its own unity, as if any analysis must disturb its beauty and its power. But he wrote the fact in actions which could never be forgotten. When his life was over, there were men and women who knew that God was just like Jesus – as loving, as holy, as full of saving and transforming power; knew, too, that at once, and before we become any better, he is willing to be our Father. In the exquisite words of R. W. Barbour, "At every step of Christ's life he let loose another secret of God's love. All God's love is in Christ. Think of every act, every event, every incident from his cradle to his grave, and you will find the Father's love stealing out somewhere."

But, he goes on, "God's love must be measured by the *whole* work of Christ." In other words – remove the Cross, and at once the revelation is lowered and impaired. For the last and highest truth about God was uttered silently at Calvary. That was the final chapter in the Son's exposition of the Father. By this death for sinners Jesus unveiled a Fatherhood of such dimensions – such breadth and length and depth and height – that sacrifice comes into it at last. The past of Old Testament religion was indeed rich in pictures and promises; yet never had grace been dreamt of so infinite as to die for man. Prophets had spoken of redemption, but the cost of redemption to God lay hid until he came upon whom it was to fall. Till Christ had been here, had come and lived and suffered, it was not known to any single soul that God loves all men – whoever they are and whatever they have done – nay more, that God has vindicated the reality and passion of his love by the endurance of vicarious pain. Nor is it until Jesus has entered our experience, revealing the blessed love of God and his communion with the sinful, that you and I can have hold of the Divine Fatherhood in a way that makes it real, near, and sure to our minds.

Some years ago the question was asked me by an earnest and able man: "What need have we of Christ? The religion of the Psalms", he added, "is enough for me." It was curiously difficult to answer him. If a man honestly feels that the faith expressed in the twenty-third Psalm, or the fifty-first, or the hundred-and-third, quite satisfies his conscience and mind and heart – how shall we then present Jesus Christ as the medium of *a new and essential gift*? Part of the answer, doubtless, is

45

that, although we may be unable to anticipate Christ as sheerly indispensable, yet we are so made that at once, when we have beheld him, we know without reasoning that he is necessary. Besides that, it may be pointed out that the Psalmists themselves are aware of deep longings and desires which their own religion could not wholly quench. With all their priceless treasures, they yet lack something. And we may go further. More and more men are conscious that we need a great fact, a reality external to self and unchanging with the centuries, on which we may ground our confidence and trust in approaching the Holy One with whom we have to do. We need, absolutely and always, a fact to which we may simply respond, which is neither the hypothesis of our reasoning nor the creation of our wishes nor the postulate of our reverent hope, but, on the contrary, a substantial and significant existence which confronts us as an irrefragable element in history, and to which our noblest aspirations and hopes can be fastened. This reality, it is plain, must needs be a Person; for only a Person can show us the personal God. We turn then to history, and there we encounter Jesus of Nazareth as the Divine answer to our human longing. Thus our question is fairly met. Do men need Christ? How is the Father known? He is known only in the Son. Only so are we *sure* of a love that saves to the uttermost, a God who is faithfully and unchangeably Redeemer.

But we may view the revelation of the Father otherwise. Try to think out carefully what you mean by God. Your mind turns immediately (does it not?) to the Divine character – the holiness, the love, the power, the eternal grace to sinners. Now when you put this down – combining it in a spiritual unity – and turn next to the picture of Christ, you discover that almost without your being aware a strange thing has occurred. Instinctively you have transferred to God those personal features, qualities, and characteristics which appear in Christ. The attributes of the Christian God, in short, are but the traits of Jesus' character exalted to infinity. Without knowing it, certainly without intending it, you have verified the Lord's own saying: "He that hath seen me hath seen the Father."

But obviously this at once creates a vast problem for the mind. Can one reveal God perfectly save he who *is* what he reveals? Apart from such real identity or unity between Revealer and Revealed, must there not be discrepancy somewhere in the revelation – an aberration or refraction of truth for which in the end we must still sadly make allowance? Prophets speak but a fragment of God's mind, for they are messengers only. But he who perfectly declares *the Father* – what is *his* place and position? No better name surely is imaginable than that which he bears throughout the writings of the New Testament – the Son of God. In will, in character, in redeeming power, he is one in person with the Eternal whose being he unfolded to the world.

Christ saves, yet only God can save. There, in a simple and elementary reflection, lies the original but also the permanent foundation of a great thought which men naturally have felt, so hard – the Divinity of Christ. It looks the merest mythology; in fact, it is but a transcript of experience. A man tries the great venture of faith. He has studied Christ in all the books. He has

sat still and thought and tried to see through his thought
the very face of Christ whom he longs to understand;
and he has not succeeded. Then he rises up for action
and resolves to seek the illumination of obedience. And
more and more as he goes his way, doing the duty,
bearing the burden, always with his eye upon the
Leader, it dawns on him that in the new life God and
Christ are morally indistinguishable. To believe in
Christ, always, is to believe in God. To do Christ's will
is to do God's will. And secretly, in the hour of
meditation, when we try to look into God's face, still
it is the face of Christ that comes up before us. Now
the man to whom this happens, if he puts intelligence
into his faith, must needs raise the last and final
question – Who *is* this marvellous Personality? Is he
but an incident of history, a wave rising on the sea of
human life, as the billows innumerable surge and melt
in mid-ocean? Is he the passing creature of time, or has
he not rather come forth out of the uncreated life of
the Eternal? Eternity or time – do we have to choose
between them? What if Christ belongs to both at once!
What if he is as old as the saving love of God, yet
emerging into history at a definite spot in the long past!
It is a paradox, of course; yet truth, we all know, may be
stranger far than fiction.

III

Jesus Christ and God

We have endeavoured in the preceding chapters to
determine the position occupied by Jesus alike in his
own message and in the experience of his Church. Our
conclusions, so far as they went, were clear enough. His
self-consciousness was unique, and he assumed a place
in the relationship of God to man which no other can
ever fill. He presented himself explicitly as the Way to
the Father. As the one essential Way, to miss which is
to miss everything worth calling life, he confronted
those who heard him with the supreme moral problem
and exerted the supreme moral authority. Advancing
next to his reality in experience, we sought to analyse
and (as it were) tabulate what he has been to men and
women who by universal consent have made Christian
history. It is an infinite theme; but we selected as fairly
typical and characteristic these three points – *first*, that
Christ is still present in full personal influence, so that
those who accept or reject him do so to his face; *second*,
that in him we attain the conquest of sin; and *finally*,
that he imparts to us a satisfying sense of God. In him

49

we see the last reality of the universe as Holy and Almighty Love.

It remains now that so far as may be we should gather up our results and give them what may be called their final meaning and direction. We proceed to ask who this extraordinary Person is, whence he came, and where in the hierarchy of spiritual being he must be placed. It is of course a long-debated point of theory; but to me at least it is questionable whether thoughtful disciples will ever consent to stand before Jesus Christ in complete silence, vetoing their own eager thought, asking no questions, working out no answers, even while all the time they are sensible of his stupendous and incomparable significance for religion. We have really no option but to think about him with all our might and with the best intellectual instruments at our command. Reason – which is more than logic – insists on coming into our faith. Nothing is easier, nothing is cheaper, and, I believe, nothing in the long result is more fatal, than to give men the impression that our religion will not bear being thought out to the end, that it dies if we bring it into the sun. The absolute and final issues created by Jesus must be faced. Now, if we regard him as Saviour, we must see him at the centre of all things. We must behold him as the pivotal and cardinal reality, round which all life and history have moved. That is a place out of which his Person simply cannot be kept. We dare not permanently live in two mental worlds, dividing the mind hopelessly against itself. We cannot indulge one day the believing view of things, for which Christ is all and in all, and the next a view of philosophy or science for which he is little or nothing or in any case ranks as quite subordinate and negligible. After all we have but one mind, which is at work both in our religion and our science; and if Christ is veritably supreme *for faith*, he is of necessity supreme altogether and everywhere. Growingly it becomes impossible to revert to a scientific or philosophical attitude in which the insight into his central greatness which we attain in moments of religious vision is resolutely and relentlessly suppressed. At every point we must be true to experience, and the deepest experience we have is our experience as believing men. Hence, if the thought of Christ we have reached is valid, it must be carried consistently up to the top and summit of being, as something which is true with a truth that will stand the closest scrutiny and verification of sympathetic minds. In this spirit let us inquire into the relation of Christ to God. If his self-consciousness is thus absolute, if he exerts this regenerating power in experience, how shall we name him best? Who *must* he be in his proper self?

Now it is worth while to accentuate the fact distinctly that at this point we are faced by a very real alternative. For we Christians are bound to place Christ either within the sphere of the Divine or without. Either he is one with the Father, or he somehow is different and unlike. Take a concrete instance, probably not uncommon, among the noblest and most magnanimous minds of our day. Here is one whose experience of Christ may be described by saying that he has turned to him for strength to do the will of God, and the required strength has been given. He has sought in him the forgiveness of sins, and in consequence the oppressive load of guilt has been lifted off, and he has obtained peace with God. Not only so; but day after day he finds that the intenser his affection for Christ and the more whole-hearted his devotion, the more swift his progress in the pursuit of righteousness. Gradually he becomes assured that Christ is superior even to conscience. While conscience may err, and has often done so, he has now learned that the will of Christ, when we are certain that we know it, is entitled to control life from end to end. If then a man has undergone these experiences, so thrilling and so revolutionary, if he recognizes them intuitively as forming part of life in its most sublime and commanding aspect, what must be his measured conviction regarding the Person through whom they have been mediated? He may say that he is prohibited by intellectual reasons from accepting the Divinity of Christ. He finds the doctrine logically or speculatively incredible. May we not suggest to him, however, that his experience being what it is such rejection can only mean that he is illegitimately isolating his intellect from the rest of life? He is declining to let his ultimate decision be controlled by the best of his knowledge and his feeling. In moments of religious vision we see deepest into the life of things and grasp most firmly the solid pillars and bases of reality; what in such high hours we know to be true regarding Jesus Christ ought therefore to determine our permanent judgment on his Person. And may we not further urge on him that already – if our description of his experience be correct – he has accepted the Divinity of our Lord *morally*, inasmuch as he has accepted it by conscience, by personal loyalty, by spiritual trust and self-committal. In words of the late Dr. Dale which once read can never be forgotten: "When the reality and greatness of his redemptive powers are known by experience, a man will have no great difficulty in believing, on the authority of the words of our Lord in the Four Gospels, that he will raise the dead and judge the world. These spiritual relations to Christ receive their intellectual interpretations in the doctrine of his divinity. The doctrine is an empty form where they are not present; and where they are present the substance of the doctrine is believed, though every theological statement of it appears to be surrounded by difficulties which make it incredible. It is an immense gain for the intellect to receive and grasp the doctrine; but the supreme thing is for Christ to be really God to the affections, the conscience, and the will. He whom I obey as the supreme authority over my life, he whom I trust for the pardon of my sins, he to whom I look for the power to live righteously, he to whose final judgment I am looking for eternal blessedness or eternal destruction, he, by whatever name I may call him, is my God. If I attribute the *name* to another, I attribute to Christ the reality for which the name stands: and unless, for me, Christ is one with the eternal, he is really above the eternal – has diviner prerogatives and achieves diviner works."

The last sentences of this extract remind us that it is possible for a man to refuse to Christ the supreme predicate of Divinity, because he is unconsciously operating with a one-sided or imperfectly ethical conception of the Divine. God – what meaning after all, belongs to that great word? What must its import be for

Christians? It means, I think, Love, Holiness, and Power
in living combination and exalted to infinity. But is it
not just this unity of qualities which we behold in
Christ? Are not these precisely the attributes in virtue
of which he subdues us to himself, forgiving all our
iniquities, evoking our obedience, and elevating the
soul triumphantly above the coward fear of things? If
then we define the term "God" in such a way as to
exclude Christ, this means – it can only mean – that
we make him *superior* to our usual thoughts of Godhead.
But if Jesus is highest in the highest realm of which we
have any knowledge, then to speak of his Divinity is
not merely natural; it is forced upon us if we wish to
express our indebtedness to him for everything which
can be called salvation. So that to call Jesus God is, in
Herrmann's words, only to give him his right name.

Let us try now to contemplate the matter from a
different point. Take the wonderful conception – be it
true or false, it at least is wonderful – that in the Person
of Christ the Almighty God has himself come amongst
us, has appeared in history "for us men and for our
salvation". And regarding this conception, let us ask
the extremely practical and incisive question: Do the
people who have to live in a world like this *require* such
a faith? Is it a faith round which they can build up a
joyous and triumphant religious life? Do they need it to
solace grief, to repel temptation, to sustain endurance,
to banish fear? In our time nothing nobler has emerged,
nothing more Christlike and fraternal, than the steady
fight against useless pain. The sense of pity is diffused
widely, so that multitudes of people steadily make a
conscience of the curable suffering of the world. They

are mostly agreed that the direst sorrows to be met with are of a mental character. They concern the spirit, not the body. When we examine ourselves, therefore, regarding our real ability to offer deliverance from the worst grief and pain, we find that the most poignant and paralysing dread of which our minds are capable is uncertainty or darkness as to the love of God. A generation since one of the most illustrious English men of science wrote as follows regarding the all but unbearable suffering involved for him in the surrender of faith in God: "I am not ashamed to confess that with this virtual negation of God the universe to me has lost its soul of loveliness; and although from henceforth the precept to 'work while it is day' will doubtless but gain an intensified force from the terribly intensified meaning of the words that 'the night cometh when no man can work', yet when at times I think, as think at times I must, of the appalling contrast between the hallowed glory of that creed which once was mine, and the lonely mystery of existence as now I find it – at such times I shall ever feel it impossible to avoid the sharpest pang of which my nature is susceptible." Total eclipse of faith in God the Father – there is nothing which cuts so deep as that, nothing which so whelms the soul in impenetrable gloom, nothing which can be compared, for hopelessness, for weakness, for power secretly to instil the dire conviction that all is vanity. Many symptoms indicate that it is very widespread at the present hour. Certain of the most sombre and powerful novels which have been written and circulated by tens of thousands in the last few years have precisely this for motive – that the universe is a death-trap, and that we men and women have been caught helplessly in the trap by a Power too great for us to control, too callous for us to soften, too far for us to reach, deaf to supplication, blind to pain. Not long since I read the following sentence in a novel of this sort at the close of a protracted scene of fatalistic tragedy. "In every hour of every day and every night", said the writer, "un-counted human creatures writhe like severed worms under the spade of chance." The author believed that. His book was written to set it forth. What shall we say to men who are in the grip of a pessimism so dark, so unrelieved? When we speak of the love of God, do they not answer, "he loves us, does he? What then has he done to prove it? It were possible to believe in a God who did something, but he does nothing. The ages pass and he gives no sign." What have we Christians to reply? Unless we *can* reply, be it remembered, we have really no Gospel. The line we employ is too short for human need.

Nor need we imagine that the sharp edge of the problem touches other people merely. Very piercingly it comes home also to ourselves. Can we forget those evil ways of which so often we are weary, while yet we have no power to forsake them? Can we forget those persistently and horribly cruel allurements which so often return upon us, torturing and confounding our best desires, depriving us of victories we had hoped to gain for good and all, till in our frailty and anguish we are fain to cry aloud that God cares nothing for our rise or fall? Surely in our own lives, though we may have escaped the fiercer outward suffering, each of us who knows the conflict of temptation is aware that we too require the assurance that the Power that made us and placed us here indeed cares for us and is acting in our checkered lot. How close in such dark hours comes the fear lest God is far way, too distant for succour, too great to observe our bitter need. "Many there be that say of my soul, There is no help for him in God."

Let us take this vast and complex fact – the fact of suffering, whether in body or in soul – and let us insist on knowing how it may be adequately met. How shall we assure men in their agony that God veritably is love? For my part, I find the one completely satisfying solution in the certainty that Christ, the Son of God, has indeed suffered in our behalf. As it has been put, "The greatest fact in the history of our world is that the Son of God became one of ourselves, and lived and died as God manifest in the flesh. Thus he translated into our human speech the language of the Eternal. He revealed in our human conditions the inmost character of God. And he did more than this, for he assured us, by the surrender of himself to humiliation and death, that God did not regard his world with callous indifference, but with deep compassion and love. The message of the Incarnation is that God loves us better than he loves himself."

Here, then, is the watchword for a conquering faith – *God was in Christ.* If – I confess the "if" is a tremendous one – if a Divine Person has been with us, living a human life, working with human hands, weeping human tears, bearing our load and carrying all our sorrows – then at once all things are changed. For then we face life, whatever it may bring of light or shadow, with hearts at rest. How St. Paul leans on this truth in the closing words of Romans viii! All the dark things have been coming back on him – tribulation, famine, nakedness, peril, sword – the whole squadron of evils striving (as it were) in unison to break down his central confidence and shroud his soul in darkness. How does he meet them? By casting himself down into the depths of the self-abnegating Divine love and staying his heart on a revealed fact: "He that spared not his own Son but delivered him up for us all." Here is what God has done. He *did*, for love's sake, all that is represented by a career in our world ending upon a cross. In this is seen the measure of a Father's love for his blinded and dying children.

It is impossible to over-estimate the practical significance and appeal of this great faith. We cannot ever exhaust the power of an eternal Love pledged to us in Christ's self-sacrifice. With this certainty in our heart, we can enter the room of the tortured invalid, or the mother mourning her dead child; we can sit by their side and say: There is love for all, for you, in God above, and what proves it is Jesus' life and Jesus' death. Do not cease to grieve; in grief there is no sin; but also do not believe that even grief is unknown to God your Father. This cup of pain you are drinking now, he also drank; in all our afflictions he was afflicted. Unless to those whom pain is breaking we can offer this Gospel, this proclamation of the love of him who came in person and shared our low condition, then we may well believe that in the last resort the problem of humanity is too much for our resources. There are fears we cannot assuage, there are griefs we cannot solace, there is darkness we cannot lighten, save by telling men in the warm accents of personal sympathy of that divine mercy which did not refuse love's last office, but stooped to suffer for the needy. Words to express this triumphant creed you may take from the New Testament or from Browning. With St. John you may say, "Herein is love, not that we loved God, but that he loved us and sent his Son." Or you may choose the modern poet's lines:

> What lacks, then, of perfection fit for God
> But just the instance which this tale supplies
> Of love without a limit? So is strength,
> So is intelligence; let love be so,
> Unlimited in its self-sacrifice;
> Then is the tale true and God shows complete.

God is no remote Deity, watching from afar a stricken world; he is a Presence and a Redeemer in our midst.

Such a train of reflection obviously dissipates one charge which has not infrequently been made against the doctrine of Christ's Divinity. It is gravely reproached with being a scholastic notion, interesting to metaphysically minded persons, but in no special connexion with practical and effective life. In all seriousness, however, can there be anything more important for life and practice than to have borne in upon us an overwhelming and sublime impression of God's love? I fancy that as we grow older, as we think longer and work harder and learn to sympathize more intelligently, the one thing we long to be able to pass on to men is a vast commanding sense of the grace of the Eternal. Compared with that, all else is but the small dust of the balance. Look at the noblest workers in the home Church, look at our missionaries over all the world; what is the inward conviction which enables them thus to

> Set up a mark of everlasting light,
> Above the howling senses' ebb and flow?

It is faith in the redeeming love of God. And that conviction, as they will tell you, they have and hold fast because they are sure that Jesus Christ is Immanuel, that he came out of the very being and bosom of God himself, and came at great cost. In him they have found the touch and breathing of the Father. It is not manuals of theology which prove this. Turn the pages of the hymn-book, and evidence of where the Church feels the centre of gravity in her creed to lie is discoverable on every side. One instance must suffice. Matthew Arnold, you remember, pronounced "When I survey the wondrous Cross" the greatest hymn in the English language. It is at least one of the greatest. Read the first lines of the second verse –

> Forbid it, Lord, that I should boast,
> Save in the death of Christ, *my God.*

Here is the ever-recurring note. From the very outset, faith has lived on the personal presence of God in Christ.

If we have moved thus far, however, it seems but reasonable to take a further step. I mean that if we are trying for a view of God's love which is really transcendent – something than which we can imagine nothing greater, because in subduing magnitude it goes beyond all we could ask or think – we seem to gain a standpoint where the idea of the pre-existence of Christ begins to count. It is an idea which of course comes up repeatedly in the New Testament – mostly by allusion, as if too familiar to every Christian to need comment or enforcing. For example, there is St. Paul's glorious verse – all the more amazing that in his argument it forms a mere aside, the careless riches (as it were) of the apostolic mind: "Ye know the grace of our Lord Jesus Christ, that, though he was rich, yet for your sakes he became poor, that ye through his poverty might be rich." Or again: "Have this mind in you, which was also in Christ Jesus: who, being in the form of God, counted it not a prize to be on an equality with God, but emptied himself, taking the form of a servant, being made in the likeness of men; and being found in fashion as a man, he humbled himself, becoming obedient unto death, yea, the death of the cross." The Apostle is speaking of the coming of Christ to earth. He is not dealing in metaphysics; he is dealing in the deepest and purest religion; and, as Bishop Gore has pointed out, what occupies his mind is not the *method* of the Incarnation, but its *motive*. He is totally absorbed and overmastered by the vision of the grace through which Christ had stooped down, so that in consequence of this un-exampled self-impoverishment we became rich, "heirs of God", as he has elsewhere said, "and joint heirs with Christ". Now this means, if it means anything, that the love embodied and conveyed in Christ were so great for his heart and imagination only because he thus caught sight of that vast background of eternal being whose glory must be sacrificed or laid aside ere Christ's earthly career had its beginning. "Any gift Christ has for me", says a modern writer, "depends on this, that he became poor. I need a God to heal the trouble of my life, but a God remote, inapprehensible, is no God for the heart. He may have all fulness of strength and wisdom and love, but if these cannot display themselves they might as well have no existence. Wisdom does not sit apart from life, but proves itself to be wisdom by entering into affairs and guiding them to worthy issues. And love, also, is no abstraction; it shows itself in loving, entering into conditions which are foreign to it in order to prove its quality. It takes upon itself burdens which are not its own, it throws aside every privilege and restriction, and plunges into the thick of common life. All that is in God could not be known without an Incarnation."

Faith, one feels, will always find it natural to echo this conviction. Doubtless the conception of Christ's pre-existence – his eternity were a better name – is one of immense difficulty. For here we light upon the enigma which in religion confronts us at every turn – the relation of eternity and time. It would scarcely be going too far to say that every statement of the doctrine of pre-existence which has ever yet been made always contains those self-contradictions, those manifest breaches of the rules of logic, which indicate that the human intellect is baffled. At the same time all will confess that various points emerge in life where, although we may not succeed in (as it were) getting our hand round a truth, *yet the truth is there*. We can feel that the dimly-perceived thought is essential for the interpretation of experience; it is apprehended even if

not comprehended. No one has explained moral freedom convincingly, yet its reality is plain. No one can
tell how or why my will contracts the muscle of my
arm, when I choose; yet the contraction happens. In
like manner one need not feel debarred by the unquestionable difficulties of the idea from taking the pre-
existence of Christ as a supremely worthy symbol and
indication of an infinite, unnameable fact. Whatever
its defects, it is at least incalculably truer than its
negation. It wonderfully assists the imagination when
we are trying to form a transcendent view of the divine
love which gave Christ, that we should realize how his
being here at all meant sacrifice, sacrifice of a kind and
magnitude which "pass understanding".

Of course it may be said with truth and point: God's
love is visible elsewhere than in Christ. Yes: it is visible
elsewhere because it exists elsewhere. It is there in the

> Relations dear, and all the charities
> Of father, son, and brother.

It is there in all high and saintly lives. Yet in contemplating such lives we scarcely feel ourselves in the
presence of Divine self-abnegation. We do not feel
that they convey Divine benefits purchased at a great
price. Such human exhibitions of love, purity, and
goodness are not such as manifestly to cost God much.
But precisely this is what we feel in Jesus. Standing in
his presence, we are conscious of "a love in God which
we do not earn, which we can never repay, but which
in our sins comes to meet us with mercy; a love which
becomes incarnate in the Lamb of God bearing the sin
of the world, and putting it away by the sacrifice of

himself". *That* means stupendous renunciation on God's part, for our sake. And this Divine acceptance of pain, dependence, shame, and death, I repeat, has gone to the world's heart. Ten thousand times it has melted down in contrition and gratitude those who must otherwise have remained stony, friendless, and despairing. In common life we well know – ofttimes we know it later with shame and unavailing sorrow – the difference between sending a sympathetic message to the suffering and going to their relief in person. Of course the analogy is incomplete and must be drawn with care; yet it does help us to form a worthy conception of something great that was in God's mind towards the world when Christ came into our midst. It marks the significant distinction between the idea of Jesus Christ on the one hand as a prophet or messenger only, and on the other hand as the Son who stooped down to identify himself with us in "an act of loving communion with our misery", that the redeeming Life might be achieved under human conditions. This is a difference which men understand perfectly; and the tone of our noblest religious conception – the conception of God as Father – is altered, subtly but unmistakably and pervasively, I believe, according as we choose the one reading of Jesus or the other.

It is not – let this be reiterated once again – it is not that God cannot be known as Love apart from his Incarnation in Christ. It is rather that, apart from Incarnation his love is not exhibited so amazingly. It does not so inspire and awe and overwhelm us. Great as the humanitarian Gospel is, we can imagine one yet greater. When I read certain modern books about Jesus

– books of a noble spirit, the authors of which one hails as brethren in faith – thought seems to travel out far and beyond all they have to offer, out to something vaster, something still more subduing. They do not make us feel that in Christ, his whole being and doing, but especially in his Cross, *God himself* is touching our lives and laying hold of us. But faith asks for the very profoundest meaning capable of being conveyed by the words, "God loves the world"; the interpretation with most *grace* in it, most of the appeal that will reach and win the guilty. And once again I suggest that when this thought of Divine Incarnation goes out of Christianity it makes a blank nothing else can fill. The scale on which God's love is manifested is changed, and can never again be quite the same. This is no mere theological refinement but a purely religious matter. A Christ who is eternal, and a Christ of whom we do not know whether he is eternal or not, are profoundly different objects, and the types of faith they respectively evoke must differ widely in horizon and in moral inspiration. If Christ grows on the soil of human nature, as simply human, we shall have to curtail our once glorious vision of the self-sacrificing love of the Eternal.

It is the standpoint furnished by Incarnation, then, which enables us to realize the quite inexpressible stake of religion in Christ's Person as an embodiment, absolute and unsurpassable, of the love of God. Let us recollect as we now conclude, that precisely this supreme interest or motive went to shape the formulation of what we call the doctrine of the Divine Trinity. There operated the same desire to see the love of God as constitutive of his very life. When men began to clear up their minds as to the implications of Jesus' self-chosen name of "Son"; when they inquired what it meant for God to be Father in his inmost being, it appeared to them that if God were Father essentially, he must be so eternally and by intrinsic nature. He did not begin to be Father perfectly when the perfect Son was born into the world. He had been Father from everlasting to everlasting, "ere the worlds began to be". But if God is Father eternally, the Christ is eternally the Son of his love, and the Father and the Son are ineffably one in the eternal perfectness of the absolute personal life. The inner life of God, before all worlds, we cannot think of save as the scene of moral and spiritual relationships – of love active, actual, and unimpeded; therefore, since we regard Christ, and also the Spirit given to testify of him, as participant in the supreme Godhead, we speak in faith of the Divine Trinity. Thus we find a home for Love in the depths of the Divine nature, "not", it has been said, "from any wanton intrusion into mysteries, but under the necessity of breaking silence". We see through a glass darkly, but the realities we discern even thus faintly are significant of the infinite richness and fulness of the life of God, who from the beginning has been sufficient unto himself.

Whatever may be said regarding this doctrine, whatever the uses to which it has been put – and not seldom they have been evil – the conception to which it points is at least a great and impressive one. Nay more, at bottom it is profoundly religious. We read again the words, "Father, glorify Thou Me with Thine own self, with the glory which I had with Thee before the world was"; and as their solemn and elusive wonder lingers on the soul we feel again how noble and subduing is that vision of the One God which beholds him as never alone, but always the Father towards whom the Son has been ever looking in the Spirit of eternal Love.

We have sought to contemplate the Lord Jesus Christ reverently in the distinct aspects of his being. We have dwelt on his attitude to men in Palestine; we have beheld him as he still speaks and lives within human souls, finally, and with a deep sense of intellectual limitation, we have sought to indicate his connexion with the inner life of God. What is the conclusion to which we have been led? Was Jesus Christ a Teacher of spiritual truth, who sealed his teaching with a noble death? That certainly, but also more. Was he the chief among the saints, who still lives on in lives made better by his timeless moral beauty? That certainly, but also more. Was he the Word of God, the transcendent message of the Creator to his creatures, breaking the aeonian silence of nature and revealing a Divine Heart in which we mortals have an inalienable place? That certainly; that beyond all doubt and question. Yet when we look onward still, we find no barrier to the veneration, the trust, the worship with which he is to be regarded. "He that hath seen Me hath seen the Father."

But let us not grow confused with many words. It is in the light of a sinner's conscience, and only there, that the fact of Christ becomes quite luminous. Within us all are two great elemental impulses, two vital and supreme desires. We crave an infinite *gift* which will satisfy even these insatiable hearts, a gift absolute, unending, eternal. We crave an infinite *object* also in which we may lose ourselves for ever and for ever. At once to take and to give in boundless measure; nothing less will satisfy the heart. These two desires are met in the Christ whom we have studied. He is the Saviour, and he is the Leader. His gifts to us are wonderful – sin pardoned, sorrow lightened, death abolished, heaven opened, and a present God in every trouble. Through him we are made personalities; no longer things, or links in a chain, but free men. But also he is the Leader, imposing on us an infinite demand. He leads us out into ever wider pastures of truth and duty, of service and self-denial from which there is no discharge, in a bond of union with himself to which even death will make no difference. All this Jesus Christ will be to you and me. Rise up and claim this Jesus for your own. Claim him, not for self merely, but for all who are dependent on your influence for their thought of life. So abide in him, the Life and Light of men, that it shall be natural for you to turn to your neighbour and your friend and say: "I have found the secret. I have found the Father. I have found the Son of Man who is also the Son of God."

Appreciation

Hugh Ross Mackintosh
Theologian of the Cross

T. F. Torrance

I first came to know Professor Mackintosh personally when in October 1934 I moved from the Faculty of Arts in the University of Edinburgh to the Faculty of Divinity, housed as it then was partly in Old College and partly in New College.* I had already become familiar with some of Mackintosh's works during my studies in classics and philosophy, and was eager to sit at his feet in preparation for the holy ministry. In New College I was more than ever drawn to his deeply evangelical and missionary outlook in theology, and to his presentation of Christ and the gospel of salvation through the cross in ways that struck home so simply and directly to the conscience of sinners. Here was a theology that matched and promised to deepen that in

* This appreciation was first published in *Scottish Bulletin of Evangelical Theology* (1987) 160–73.

which I had been brought up by my missionary parents. I was far from being disappointed. To study with H. R. Mackintosh was a spiritual and theological benediction, for he was above all a man of God, full of the Holy Spirit and of faith. His exposition of biblical and evangelical truth in the classical tradition of the great patristic theologians and of the Reformers was as lucid as it was profound, but it was always acutely relevant, for the central thrust of the Christian message was brought to bear trenchantly and illuminatingly upon the great movements of thought that agitated the modern world. We were made to see everything in the light of the revelation of God's infinite love and grace in Jesus Christ and of the world mission of the gospel. How frequently he used to refer to "a vast and commanding sense of the Grace of the Eternal"!

I shall never forget the teaching of Professor Mackintosh in the academic session of 1935–36 during the course on Christian Dogmatics which he gave New College students in their second year. It was a basic course which covered all the main doctrines of the faith. The central bulk of it had to do with Christology and soteriology, but the nerve of it all was the forgiveness of sins provided directly by God in Jesus Christ at infinite cost to himself. It is at this point, Mackintosh felt, that everything becomes crucial, for that is where the real nature of the Triune God becomes disclosed to us as through the reconciling sacrifice of the Son and in one Spirit we are given access to the Father and come to apprehend him in accordance with what he is in himself, even though what he is in his Triune Being infinitely transcends our comprehension.

During the previous academic session, 1934–35, Mackintosh's lectures had made an unusually disturbing and profound impact, and we became aware in the College that a theological revolution was in process, clearly evident in the excitement and transformation of our seniors. This must undoubtedly be linked with the impact upon New College of the First half-volume of Karl Barth's *Church Dogmatics, The Doctrine of the Word of God*, which had just been translated by G. T. Thomson and published in Edinburgh by T&T Clark. This had the effect of reinforcing the strong biblical and incarnational emphasis of H. R. Mackintosh in which he had anticipated Barth's reaction to the liberal teaching of Ritschl and Schleiermacher. No one could accuse Mackintosh of not giving careful attention to Ritschl and Schleiermacher, for along with A. B. Macaulay and J. S. Stewart he had been responsible for making their greatest works available in English, so that the welcome he gave to Barth's *Dogmatics* was something that could not be ignored. It was he above all who encouraged us to study the theology of Barth, for criticize it as we might, it was nonetheless "the Christian thinking of a great Christian mind of incalculable import for the Church of our time".

It soon became clear that through this alliance of the Christian dogmatics of H. R. Mackintosh with the Church dogmatics of Karl Barth something of great importance had begun to take place among us – the essential status of evangelical dogmatics as the pure science of theology was being rehabilitated at a level that the Church in Scotland had not witnessed since the end of the First World War. As Mackintosh used to teach us, dogmatics is not the systematic study of the sanctioned dogmas of the Church, but the elucidation of the full content of revelation, of the Word of God as contained in Holy Scripture, and as such is concerned with the intrinsic and permanent truth which Church doctrine in every age is meant to express. It is "systematic" only in the sense that every part of Christian truth is vitally connected with every other part. No doctrine can be admitted which does not bring to expression some aspect of the redemption that is in Christ. Thus for Mackintosh as for Barth it is in Christ alone that the truth of dogmatics finds its organic unity. There is no knowledge of Christ apart from his truth and no knowledge of his truth apart from Christ, for he himself is the co-efficient of his doctrine. Thus seriously to study Christian dogmatics was from beginning to end an empirical encounter and a personal engagement with the tangible reality of Jesus Christ. Properly pursued in this way dogmatic theology becomes "the conscience of the Church".

It was Mackintosh's habit to give out to his students at the beginning of each class one or two sheets in which he presented in succinct paragraphs the contents of the lecture he was about to give. These were doubtless revised from time to time, but in the lectures of 1935–36 he was often very unhappy with what he gave us. He would ask us to strike out certain paragraphs and put a question mark to others – I think particularly here of his lectures on the nature, origin and diffusion of sin. Some days he would come into the lecture room clearly troubled as though still wrestling in his mind and soul with the truth which he sought to express, but on other days he would come mastered by profound serenity of spirit which was almost awesome as we were ushered through his teaching into the presence of God. The lectures he gave us were often a form of what St. Paul called *logike latreia*, "rational worship". And they were always evangelical and redemptive in their import. Many a would-be theological student was converted in his classes, although some, as I well remember, used to get very angry for they found themselves questioned down to the bottom of their being. Mackintosh was immensely modest and never arrogant, but he left no room for compromise in the way his lectures drew us out under the searching light of the holy love of God incarnate in Christ. Mackintosh himself was so consumed with the moral passion of the Father revealed in the death of Jesus on the cross, that in his lecture-room we often felt we were in a sanctuary where the holiness and nearness of God were indistinguishable.

When Professor Mackintosh died in June that year (1936), I was devastated. I had been wandering about the Middle East so that news of his death took some time to reach me. He and his teaching meant so much to me that suddenly New College seemed quite empty. As I asked myself what I had learned from him my thoughts kept returning to the unconditional grace of God freely poured out upon us in Jesus Christ his incarnate Son at infinite cost to himself. *The Doctrine of the Person of Jesus Christ* and *The Christian Experience of Forgiveness*, his two major works, undoubtedly enshrine the main substance of his incarnational theology which he consistently presented from a soteriological perspective. The primary emphasis was on the supreme truth that it is none other than God himself who has come among us in Jesus Christ, and who in the crucifixion of his incarnate Son has taken the whole burden of our sin and guilt directly upon himself – all in such a way that the passionate holy love of God the Father enacts both the judgment of sin and the forgiveness of the sinner.

As a young man Mackintosh had studied in Freiburg, Halle, and then in Marburg where he became greatly indebted and attached to Wilhelm Herrmann, and where he laid the foundation for his unparalleled knowledge of German Lutheran and Reformed theology, not least of Ritschl and Schleiermacher and some of their illustrious disciples like Martin Kähler. He was drawn to the Christ-centred emphasis on experience which he found in Schleiermacher, for it rang bells in his own Highland evangelical religion; and he was drawn to the moral emphasis of Ritschl, for it rang bells in his own moral passion derived from his Scottish Calvinism. Right from the start, however, Mackintosh felt compelled to operate primarily with ontological, rather than with psychological or ethical categories, in his understanding of Jesus Christ, for the very essence of divine revelation and the very substance of the gospel of salvation were at stake. Thus we find him insisting again and again that if the revelation of God in the New Testament is true, Jesus Christ must be in himself what he reveals; and if the New Testament message of salvation is true, what Jesus Christ does for us must be what God himself does. Christians are bound to place Christ either within the sphere of the Divine or without. Either he is one with the Father or he somehow is different and unlike. Apart from a real identity or unity between the revealer and revealed, revelation suffers from a fatal discrepancy, and apart from a real incarnation Christianity suffers from a blank which nothing else can fill. Hence with reference to Matthew 11:27 or Luke 10:22 or John 5:27, like Athanasius and the Nicene theologians, Mackintosh laid constant emphasis upon the unique, incomparable and unshared connexion in knowing and being and act between the Son and the Father. As he used to express it in his lectures. "When I look into the face of Jesus Christ and see the face of God, I know that I have not seen that face elsewhere and could not see it elsehow, for he and the Father are one." It was thus that his appropriation of the Nicene *homoousion*, or oneness in being with the Father, constituted the corner-stone of H. R. Mackintosh's Christology and soteriology. Judged from that standpoint he found the concepts of divine revelation in the theologies of Schleiermacher and Ritschl to be very weak and inadequate, and their conceptions of the gospel to be evangelically and soteriologically seriously deficient.

Mackintosh never shrank from the ontological implications of this high Christology. Thus in an early work of 1912, *The Person of Jesus Christ*, he argued that if Jesus is God incarnate, then we must think of him consistently and strictly in accordance with "the constitution of his being". We are bound to think of him, therefore, as constituting "the hinge and pivot of the universe, the Person on whom everything turned in the relation of God to man". In fact the last foundations of being were in him. That is how Mackintosh interpreted the Messianic role ascribed to Jesus. "All creation in heaven and on earth, all the divine ways of history, all time and eternity – they meet and converge in this one transcendent Figure." Moreover, if Jesus Christ is on the divine side of reality, then we really have no option but to think about him with all our might and with the best intellectual instruments at our command. "Reason which is more than logic – insists on coming into our faith." Thus Mackintosh would have nothing to do with the Ritschlian conception of faith as an attitude of mind entirely independent of reason. On the contrary, we are obliged before God to use our reason in thinking out to the end the absolute and final issues constituted by Jesus. "If we regard him as Saviour, we must see him at the centre of all things. We must behold him as the pivotal and cardinal reality, round which all life and history have moved." That is a place, Mackintosh went on to argue, out of which his Person simply cannot be kept.

> We dare not permanently live in two mental worlds, dividing the mind hopelessly against itself. We cannot indulge one day the believing view of things, for which Christ is all and in all, and the next a view of philosophy or science for which he is little or nothing or in any case ranks as quite subordinate and negligible. After all we have but one mind, which is at work both in our religion and our science; and if Christ is veritably supreme *for faith*, he is of necessity supreme altogether and everywhere. It becomes increasingly impossible to revert to a scientific or philosophical attitude in which the insight into his central greatness which we attain in moments of religious vision is resolutely and relentlessly suppressed. At every point

we must be true to experience, and the deepest experience we
have is our experience as believing men. Hence, if the thought
of Christ we have reached is valid, it must be carried consistently up to the top and summit of being, as something
which is true with a truth that will stand the closest scrutiny
and verification of sympathetic minds.

It was precisely on these Christological grounds, and
because of the unity of redemption and creation and of
faith and reason which they implied, that Mackintosh
strenuously rejected the rigid dualism that had been
injected into Western thought through the rationalism
and determinism of Enlightenment science and philosophy. Thus he constantly objected to the tendency in
modern thought, found even in Christian forms, to cut
the universe in two halves, one physical and the other
spiritual, and thereafter to argue that a mechanically
constituted system of laws rules in the first half, but not
in the second. Here the notion of a closed mechanistic
universe had been allowed to interpose itself between
man and God with a deistic and secularizing effect. It
shut off the world of matter from God, and caged human
beings within the prison of inexorable "laws of nature",
thus suffocating thoughts of prayer and miracle and the
free interaction of God and mankind.

For Mackintosh such a closed deterministic conception of the universe conflicted sharply with the nature
of God the Father revealed in the incarnation of his
Son, and our understanding of the omnipotence,
providential ubiquity, accessibility, and freedom of God
to protect and save his children. Thus, along with his
colleague Professor Daniel Lamont, who in earlier life
had been an assistant to Lord Kelvin, Mackintosh

welcomed the concept of a time-dependent universe, advocated scientifically by Einstein and philosophically by Bergson, which through its inherent properties was open to the future and not closed. Yet it was not on scientific or philosophical grounds that Mackintosh himself took his stand, so much as on the irrefragable conviction that a mechanistic explanation of the universe conflicted sharply with the essential nature of God the Creator and Redeemer revealed in the life, death and resurrection of Jesus Christ. But it did mean for Mackintosh that an obligation is laid upon the believer to think out to the very end the bearing of the Father's immeasurable love upon the whole universe of visible and invisible reality, in which it would be quite inadmissible to hold theological, scientific and philosophical conceptualities completely apart from each other.

Now if faith places Christ on the divine side of reality, as perfectly of one being with God, how are we to understand the incarnation and the cross? It was in connexion with that question that kenotic theory had been brought into prominence in attempts to harmonize the deity of Christ with his life and work within the limitations of human existence and suffering in space and time. Mackintosh, however, while giving the kenotic conception sympathetic consideration in its reference to the self-humiliation of God, would have nothing to do with any metaphysical speculation about an emptying of divine attributes in the incarnation, for God could not be thought of as emptying anything out of his own essential being as God. *Kenosis* was rather to be understood as the sell-emptying of God himself into

our frail contingent existence but our estranged
condition under the condemnation of his eternal truth
and righteousness. That is to say, *kenosis* has to be
understood as the utterly astonishing and incompre-
hensible act of God's self-humiliation and self-
abnegating love in which he freely made himself one
with us in our actual existence in order to share the
shame of our sin and guilt and through atoning sacrifice
to effect our salvation. For Mackintosh, then, the
concept of *kenosis*, religiously and soteriologically
understood, was not to be taken as an explanation of
"how" the incarnation took place, but as the almighty
act of God in surrendering himself to humiliation and
death in order to forgive our sins – it was a revelation
of the inexhaustible power of God's love. It was in
fact another way of expressing the grace of the Lord
Jesus Christ who for our sakes became poor that we
through his poverty might become rich. Jesus Christ is
God with us, Immanuel, who coming out of the very
being and bosom of God, and at such infinite cost,
constitutes in himself the message that "*God loves us
better than he loves himself*"!

Mackintosh could never refer to the cross of Christ
without an instinctive feeling of awe and wonder at the
forgiveness of sins effected in it by the incredible act of
God's atoning self-sacrifice. He had no hesitation in
speaking of the death of Christ as the central fact in
the whole history of God's relations with the world, for
in it God interposed himself in the utterly impossible
predicament of his alienated children in order to break
the power of sin and guilt and redeem mankind from its
tyranny. The forgiveness of sins was for Mackintosh the

greatest of all miracles, the wonder of wonders. It was the supreme instance of God's omnipotent Love. What he found so breath-taking in the forgiveness of sins was the conjunction of the infinite holiness and the infinite love of God manifested in it. Divine forgiveness carries in its heart the complete exposure, rejection and condemnation of sin through the self-maintaining reaction of God's very nature as God, and yet it is the utterly inexplicable act in which God in his unfathomable love has taken that fearful judgment of our sin upon himself and paid the price of our redemption. In the forgiveness of sins enacted in the crucifixion of Jesus the holiness and nearness of God, the judgment and love of God, are inextricably woven together. "The passion of God is there." Hence it is made clear that "none can pardon sin ultimately, save he who expiates it, and through whose experience of pain the costly gift is mediated. Thus the Cross which detects the sin reveals also the love of God."

It was characteristic of Mackintosh's personal appreciation of the staggering truth of divine forgiveness, not just as a gracious declaration of pardon, but as a mighty act of God, that he should have entitled his book about it *The Christian Experience of Forgiveness*. The Gospels tell us that even before his death and resurrection it, was, the supreme prerogative of Jesus to impart forgiveness, to put it right into the heart of men and women in such a way that it became "an experimental truth" in their lives. Thus Mackintosh could say of Christ: "He saved men by his filial life even before he saved them by self-sacrifice in his death." How much more with the fulfilment of his redemptive mission! The incarnate presence and activity of God himself in the life, death and resurrection of Jesus, is not just the greatest fact of all history but remains throughout all history as the supreme empirical event confronting and challenging human beings through the gospel. Jesus Christ risen from the dead, with the virtue of his atoning death in him for ever, and therefore embodying the forgiveness of sins, continually steps out of the pages of history, a tremendous, and exacting reality, creatively evoking from human beings an evangelical experience of forgiveness that answers to the very experience of God himself in mediating it through the sacrifice of Calvary. It was thus that Mackintosh could speak so vividly of the "experienced", "felt" or "tangible" reality of Christ as Lord and Saviour, and could not but interpret everything in the New Testament gospel in accordance with the commanding impact of that reality upon his mind and heart.

The Christian experience of forgiveness, however, is not simply the experience of an external relation to the cross to be interpreted in moral terms. In line with his rejection of Ritschlian moral categories for ontological categories in his understanding of the Person of Christ, Mackintosh held, with Calvin, that we partake of all his saving benefits only as we are united to him. Thus, in contrast to his colleague James Denney in Glasgow who interpreted St. Paul's doctrine of union with Christ only in moral or judicial terms, Mackintosh operated with a conception of a spiritual and personal union with Christ that goes far beyond anything that human beings can experience with one another, for it involves a relation of mutual indwelling and spiritual coalescence between Christ and his people. Mackintosh was undoubtedly influenced here by his old teacher, Wilhelm Herrmann, whose book *Communion with God* he urged all his students to study closely. Herrmann taught that the Christian lives through sharing in "the inner life of Jesus" in which he finds his own life becoming spiritually subdued in conformity to the historic life of Jesus. However, Mackintosh differed radically from Herrmann in the latter's exclusion of the resurrection from "the historic Jesus", which meant that Herrmann's notion of union with Christ could be interpreted finally as little more than a sharing in the spiritual convictions of Jesus. For Mackintosh, on the other hand, the resurrection must be included in the entire empirical fact of Christ so that to share in the inner life of Jesus means to be united to him in the wholeness of his incarnate reality as the crucified and risen Son of God. This must include, in some real measure, an intimate assimilation into that inner life through sharing in the power of Christ's resurrection, and with constant reference to his self-consciousness as reflected in the Gospels and the impression it made upon the first Christians.

Mackintosh's soteriological restatement of the *unio mystica* as an empirical truth derived not a little support from the teaching of John McLeod Campbell, with whom also he shared an approach to the understanding of Christ and the atonement in terms of the inner relations between the incarnate Son and the Father, and therefore of the direct action of God upon sinful humanity. Although he was somewhat critical of what he called McLeod Campbell's notion of "vicarious penitence of Christ", Mackintosh agreed with him in refusing to separate the incarnation from the atonement, and thus in declining to offer a doctrine of atonement in terms of a merely *external* moral or judicial transaction between God and sinners, as though Christ's righteousness and our guilt were both externally transferable. Far from rejecting the forensic element in the atoning and propitiatory work of Christ, however, he interpreted it as falling within the inner being of Jesus in terms of his active as well as his passive obedience under the judgment of divine holiness and love. The rendering of atonement is to be understood, then, in terms of the inward experience of the incarnate Son in a profound union with sinners in the actualities of their alienated existence and fearful perdition – "My God, my God why hast thou forsaken me?" – whereby he took completely upon himself shame and responsibility for their sin and guilt in acceptance of the righteous judgment of the Father, but all in unbroken union with the Father and in perfect identity in will and mind with his condemnation of sin. Thus in his atoning life and death Jesus Christ realized directly in his own profound experience as the obedient Son the unspeakable pain and infinitely costly experience of the Father in the mediation and actualization of forgiveness. The ultimate stress in Mackintosh's doctrine of atonement was definitely upon the immediate act of God in the vicarious passion of Christ, and thus upon the inseparable and inherent relation between the judgment and love of God. Of absolutely essential and crucial significance, therefore, was the link between the atonement and the divinity of Christ, apart from which the cross of Christ could not be understood as the final revelation of divine love or as the ultimate disclosure given to mankind of the inner nature of God the Father Almighty, who not only made all things visible and invisible but whose providence unceasingly overrules and directs the whole course of events in the universe.

In his doctrine of atonement Mackintosh was also clearly influenced by the ontological understanding of it offered by the great Greek Fathers, evident in their soteriological principle that "the unassumed is the unhealed", to which he frequently referred. That is to say, the incarnation itself, and indeed the whole incarnate life of the Son of God, as Calvin also taught, must be regarded as redemptive and saving event reaching its great climax in the crucifixion and resurrection, in which God in Jesus Christ penetrated into the dark depths of our fallen and enslaved humanity in order to break the hold of sin and guilt entrenched within us by atoning expiation, and to redeem us by the power of his endless life in his resurrection from the grave. The fruit of that atoning emancipation is the forgiveness of sins, but precisely because of the oneness of the incarnation and the atonement, and of the person and the work of Christ, divine forgiveness is for ever embodied in the Person of the crucified and risen Jesus and becomes empirically ours in a profound union with him effected in us through faith by the indwelling Spirit of God.

At an earlier point reference was made to the awesome fact, constantly pointed out by Mackintosh, that in the very heart of the divine act of forgiveness there is a profound conjunction of the utter holiness and the infinite love of God. The unconditional self-giving of God in love to the sinner in the sacrificial death of Jesus carried intrinsically with it the absolute rejection by that love of the inconceivable wickedness for which Jesus came to make atoning expiation on the cross. It is there in the cross that the gravity of sin is revealed. Thus it may be said on the one hand that God's inexorable opposition to sin is exhibited as much in forgiveness as in judgment, and on the other hand that God's holiness has a redemptive as well as a condemnatory aspect, and indeed that his judgment is finally a manifestation and instrument of his grace. "Grace means that in his loving self-bestowal his severity is absorbed, yet does not disappear. It is a stringent love, and by being less stringent God would become not more loving but less Divine." It was in this light that Mackintosh taught us to think of the wrath of God as the obverse of the moral passion of his love when he stooped down to suffer on behalf of men and bring them forgiveness at unspeakable cost to himself; and it was always on this ground that he exposed the moral superficiality and soteriological deficiency of any attempt to eliminate the notion of wrath from the doctrine of God. "In sober truth, it is only the man who knows what grace is that can tell what wrath and judgment are." He used to tell us that he never forgot that day in Marburg when he heard Herrmann say that Ritschl's attempt to expel the conception of God's wrath against sin from theology was itself a great sin against the Christian mind. I imagine also that it was for this reason that the very first essay he asked us to write for him was one on the wrath of God.

Let me now refer back again to those lectures which Professor Mackintosh gave us in the Spring of 1936, in which his thought was so clearly engaged in a process of transition. What was actually going on in his mind? I think I began to understand at least a little of what was involved when in the following year I read and reread his last book *Types of Modern Theology*, which was, so to speak, his last will and testament to us. In it we were given in an expanded form his Croall Lectures which he had first delivered in 1933, but which he had been revising each year as he read them again to his senior class. They were prepared for publication by his close friend Professor A. B. Macaulay, who tells us that all but the last thirteen pages had been given their final revision by Mackintosh before his death on 8 June 1936. Macaulay, who had recently retired from Trinity College in Glasgow, had been lecturing in New College in place of Professor Daniel Lamont during the latter's absence on Moderatorial duties, in the Kirk. When Mackintosh died, Macaulay, who was not so sympathetic to Barth as Mackintosh, took over his classes until Professor G. T. Thomson joined us from Aberdeen.

Types of Modern Theology is a profound and brilliant work revealing a remarkable mastery of the history of modern thought. In it Mackintosh offered a penetrating analysis of the dominant theologies of the nineteenth and twentieth centuries associated with Schleiermacher, Hegel, Ritschl, Troeltsch, Kierkegaard and Barth. Again and again he found the gospel itself to have been precariously in balance as people of admittedly great intellectual stature sought to interpret it within prevailing cultural patterns of thought alien to it and the biblical thought-forms in which it has been mediated to us. Along with his shrewd epistemological questions, he put to them the searching questions with which he was wont to test every theology: How far is it rooted in God's self-revelation in Jesus Christ? Can it be preached to sinful people in need of forgiveness? How effective will it be in the mission field? "The message that does not evangelize, the Christianity that does not convert, abroad or at home, cannot be true."

Mackintosh did not evade the great philosophical or critical issues with which these continental theologies had wrestled in seeking to commend Christianity to modern culture, for he handled them with a generous sympathy and respect, but he was as relentless as he was rigorous in assessing the justice they did to the absoluteness of the divine initiative in revelation and the uniqueness of God's identification with mankind in the incarnation. The judgments he passed upon their evangelical and soteriological inadequacy were judgments, he felt, which could not but be passed by a mind that has submitted trustfully to divine revelation in Jesus Christ. Søren Kierkegaard and especially Karl Barth, to whom Mackintosh devoted a third of the book, clearly measured up best to his theological scrutiny. His trenchant handling of their thought was not without sharp criticism – this was particularly the case with Kierkegaard, though not always, I think, with sufficient understanding of his real intention – but his warm appreciation of the fundamental change in theological outlook to which they contributed so powerfully showed the direction in which Mackintosh's own thought was moving.

It was, I believe, in the course of revising *Types of Modern Theology* and particularly in coming to terms with Karl Barth's theology of the Word of God, that Mackintosh was forced to think through his own theological convictions in a more radical way than ever before. Thus he allowed his own judgments on nineteenth-century theology, especially on Schleiermacher and Ritschl, to reflect back upon himself, and at the same time he asked how far his own theological position stood up to the challenge of Karl Barth in his criticism, exaggerated though it sometimes appeared to be, of the whole development of Protestant thought since the Reformation in allowing the preaching and teaching of the gospel to be compromised by humanism and secularism. Mackintosh's own commitment to a thoroughly biblical, evangelical and Christocentric stance in preaching and teaching alike made him appreciative of but also sensitive to Barth's penetrating exposure of the hidden and subtle ways in which even a Christocentric approach can be betrayed from below.

Three aspects of Mackintosh's own thought, as I think he came to realize, were open, at least in some measure, to Barth's critique. Let me hasten to add, however, that they were all aspects in which Mackintosh had clearly anticipated Barth: in his stress upon the divine initiative, his biblical understanding of sin, and his conception of the uniqueness of divine revelation.

According to Mackintosh it is a conspicuous feature of the Christian faith that in his grace God always takes the initiative with us and maintains that initiative in all his relations with us. However, he had been in the habit of linking this to an innate hunger or craving or need of man for God which he held to be "a true point of contact for the gospel of Jesus Christ – a point of contact not created by man but kept in being by God". Although he claimed that Christian faith does nothing so silly as to turn these human cravings into an explanation of religion itself, he could nevertheless argue that to some extent we may tell what must in general be the character of the Reality that will adequately evoke and satisfy those cravings or needs. It was precisely to such a line of thought (the deadly *analogia entis*!) that Barth traced the subtle naturalism that had steadily corrupted and compromised the gospel in Germany – a point which Mackintosh must have taken to heart, if only through his own analysis of the religious notions of Hegel and Troeltsch, making him develop even further his own emphasis on the originality and absoluteness of Christianity and the danger of allowing our understanding of revelation and grace to be trapped in "nature".

Nowhere had Professor Mackintosh been more critical of himself than in respect of his lecture summaries on sin, to which I alluded earlier. As I look back upon these, what strikes me is that they were written with too much attention to the philosophical and moral and even evolutionary accounts of evil that had come to prevail in Protestant theology since Kant. As such they did not match up to Mackintosh's profound understanding of the infinite moral passion of God in the atonement or to his account of the utter exposure and judgment of sin in the cross of Christ and its enactment of forgiveness. But that was, as far as I recall, the way in which Mackintosh lectured on the nature of sin in spite of what he had written beforehand. I can still hear him say, "At Holy Communion I feel ashamed for my whole being, for my good as well as for my evil." Kierkegaard's sharp distinction in *Fear and Trembling* and in *Training in Christianity* between an ethical and a religious (that is a distinctively Christian) view of sin had clearly struck home to Mackintosh and chimed in completely with his dominant soteriological perspective. Moreover, from Barth he learned to think again of the profound antagonism of sin that is deeply ingrained in the human reason and which constantly assumed deceptive "moral" and "religious" forms. It was doubtless the radical nature of Barth's doctrine of justification that influenced Mackintosh here and threw him back more squarely onto his own understanding of the judgment of the unconditional grace of God upon the whole being of man.

In his analyses of modern thought Mackintosh charged it again and again with a weak sense of revelation, which he traced back to a dualist outlook deriving from Enlightenment rationalism in which God was shut off from all direct action in the empirical world. He used to point to a very different view of God held by D. S. Cairns of Aberdeen, who thought of the kingdom of God as providentially and triumphantly intervening even in the realm of nature which mechanistic science claimed as its own exclusive reserve. An "unerring" criterion Mackintosh used to apply in this connexion was the view a theologian had

of "petitionary prayer", but he also sought to determine how he reacted to the "incomparable majesty of
the Bible". Thus he would ask whether a theologian's
method was to proceed by introspection or self-
understanding rather than by listening to the voice of
God speaking in his Word. It is understandable,
therefore, that Mackintosh was instinctively drawn to
the supreme truth upon which all Barth's theology
turned, that God himself is the content of his revelation, and therefore that the incarnational revelation of
God as Father, Son and Holy Spirit must be regarded as
grounded in eternal ontological relations in the
Godhead. *Ab initio* God is revealed as Father, Son and
Holy Spirit. This meant that what God is toward us in
his Word he is inherently and eternally in himself, and
thus that in the Word of God it is none other than God
himself that he communicates to us. Not only is it the
case that the eternal Word is the *prius* of revelation; in
actual fact the Word of God is Jesus Christ, and it is he,
the incarnate Word, who is mediated to us through the
witness of the Holy Scriptures. The effect upon
Mackintosh of this Trinitarian doctrine of the Word of
God was to impart new ontological and objective depth
and greater concreteness to his conception of divine
revelation through the Bible, which is already evident
not only in his concluding chapter on Karl Barth but
throughout all his discussion in *Types of Modern
Theology*.

There is one further point which I must mention in
my recollection of H. R. Mackintosh, the profound
interrelation he cultivated between preaching and
teaching the gospel. This was particularly evident in

his quite unforgettable "sermon class" in which, through unsparing yet sympathetic criticism of the sermons we prepared, he instructed us how to let them arise out of a thorough exegesis of the Scripture and to work out for ourselves how we might best speak the Word of the gospel directly to the human heart. I think here particularly of the simple and direct messages he composed so effectively for distribution as evangelical tracts in *The Monthly Visitor*. They were Mackintosh's counterpart to Barth's later sermons to prisoners, but were evangelically directed to the "alarmed conscience" of sinners in a rather more telling and personal way. He once published, through Drummond's Tract Depot in Stirling, a beautiful pamphlet entitled *The Heart of the Gospel and the Preacher*, which is all about the place that must be given to the atonement both as the central truth and as the permanent undertone of all preaching. "Without preaching the Atonement we can never satisfy the conscience or heart of man." "Assured reconciliation was beyond hope until Jesus, bearing in Himself the very grace and life of God, numbered Himself with the transgressors and took our burdens as His own." There in his own words we have expressed for us the essence of the faith of Hugh Ross Mackintosh, and the central nerve of all his theology.